THE BRAZILIANS
HOW THEY LIVE AND WORK

The Brazilians
HOW THEY LIVE AND WORK

R. A. Wellington

DAVID & CHARLES
NEWTON ABBOT   LONDON
NORTH POMFRET (VT)   VANCOUVER

0 7153 6581 9

Set in 11pt Baskerville, 2pt leaded
and printed in Great Britain
by Latimer Trend & Company Ltd Plymouth
for David & Charles (Holdings) Limited
South Devon House Newton Abbot Devon

Published in the United States of America
by David & Charles Inc
North Pomfret Vermont 05053 USA

Published in Canada
by Douglas David & Charles Limited
3645 McKechnie Drive West Vancouver BC

Contents

Contents

List of Illustrations

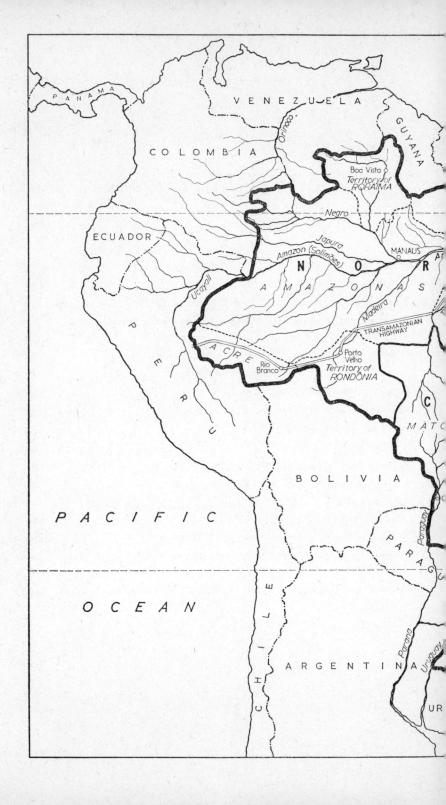

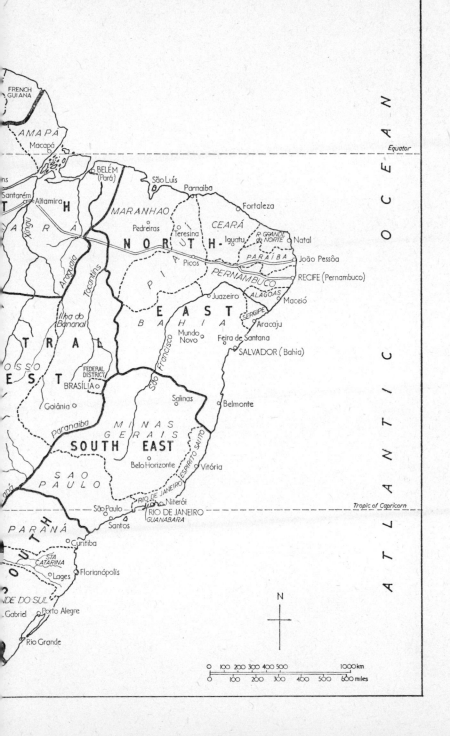

FRENCH
GUIANA

AMAPA

Macapá

ins

Santarém
Altamira

X̄ı̄ngu̇

Araguaia

Tocantins

N O R T H

MARANHAO

BELÉM
(Pará)

São Luís

Parnaíba

Fortaleza

Pedreiras

Teresina

CEARÁ

Iguatú

R. GRANDE
NORTE

Natal

Picos

PARAÍBA

João Pessôa

PERNAMBUCO

RECIFE (Pernambuco)

P I A U Í

Juazeiro

ALAGOAS

Maceió

E A S T

B A H I A

SERGIPE

Aracaju

Ilha do
Bananal

Mundo
Novo

Feira de Santana

SALVADOR (Bahia)

T R A L

OSSO

E S T

FEDERAL
DISTRICT

BRASÍLIA

Goiânia

Paranaiba

Salinas

Belmonte

M I N A S
G E R A I S

São Francisco

ESPIRITO SANTO

SOUTH   EAST

Belo Horizonte

Vitória

S A O
P A U L O

RIO DE JANEIRO

Niterói

aá

São Paulo

Santos

RIO DE JANEIRO
GUANABARA

Tropic of Capricorn

PARANÁ

Curitiba

STA
CATARINA

Lages

Florianópolis

UTH

DE DO SUL

Gabriel

Porto Alegre

Rio Grande

N

A T L A N T I C

O C E A N

Equator

0   100 200 300 400 500   1000 km
0   100   200   300   400   500   600 miles

Introduction

THE difficulty of writing a topical book with facts and figures about Brazil is that statistics are practically out of date by the time the ink has dried on them, such is the present rate at which the country is developing. This applies especially to population, production of manufactures, and foreign trade figures as well as to exchange rates.

From being for many years a traditional exporter of coffee and raw materials, Brazil is rapidly establishing itself as a producer of manufactured goods and, through an aggressive sales policy, is finding growing outlets for them abroad. It is only a question of time before packing cases labelled 'made in Brazil' will be seen on docksides all over the world. This is a far cry from the days, not so long ago, when Brazil was known merely as 'the land where the nuts come from'.

Referred to (usually ironically) in the past as 'the country of the future', Brazil has suddenly found its feet in the present and the result is as exciting for most Brazilians as it is for foreigners like myself who have been associated with the country and its people for a lifetime. Those of us who have a deep-rooted affection for Brazil and the Brazilians cannot fail to be happily impressed by the great progress made by the country during recent years nor can we hide our satisfaction that its people now seem to be well set on the road to prosperity through the introduction of sound and forward-looking economic and social policies.

Note on exchange rates It is not easy to keep up to date with

exchange rates owing to the Brazilian policy of frequent
devaluations of the cruzeiro. Devaluations of the pound sterling
and of the US dollar have complicated matters even further so
far as conversion figures in this book are concerned. The following official conversion rates quoted in Brazil on 6 December
1973 may serve as a general guide:

US dollar—buying rate 6·120 cruzeiros
Pound sterling—buying rate 14·22 cruzeiros

Note also   Billion = 1,000 millions.

I

The Country and the People

THE federative republic of Brazil, referred to hereafter simply as Brazil, covers an area of 3,286,470 square miles and is the fifth largest country in the world, being exceeded in size only by Canada, China, the USA and the USSR. Brazil is about thirty-five times larger than the UK. At its extremes the country measures 2,684 miles from north to south and 2,689 miles from east to west. Brazil's seaboard extends for 4,630 miles along the Atlantic Ocean. The country lies between latitudes 5° 16′19″ N and 33° 45′09″ S and longitudes 34° 45′54″ E and 73° 59′32″ W, nine-tenths of Brazilian territory being between the Equator and the Tropic of Capricorn. Brazil has common frontiers with all other South American countries except Chile and Ecuador. The country is similar in shape to the South American continent and covers 47 per cent of its total area.

Brazil is divided into twenty-two states, four federal territories and the federal district in which the capital city of Brasilia is situated. Some of the states are gigantic. That of Mato Grosso, for instance, covers 475,503 square miles and is larger than Belgium, France, the Netherlands, Portugal and Spain combined. The state of Minas Gerais covers 225,975 square miles and is bigger than France. The largest state of Brazil is Amazonas. Covering 601,927 square miles, it is bigger than Alaska and more than twice the size of Texas. Yet the population of Amazonas in 1970 was roughly equivalent to that of

Rhode Island and the population of Mato Grosso about the same as that of Northern Ireland.

The country presents a great variety of climate, vegetation, physical characteristics and natural resources. More than half of Brazil's territory has an elevation of less than 1,000ft. The highest point is the Pico da Neblina (Misty Peak), which reaches 9,889ft and is on the northern frontier with Venezuela. Some of the best known of Brazil's great rivers are the Amazon, the Paraná and the São Francisco. Draining 440 million cu ft per minute, the 4,050 mile long Amazon is the mightiest river in the world. More than a third of the country is taken up by the vast Amazon basin in which there is a huge area of forest, much of it still unexplored. Roads are now being built through this region to establish land communication with cities like Manaus which until recently could be reached only by river or by air. Most of the drained area of the Amazon basin lowland has an elevation of less than 800ft and the rainfall, though heavy in some parts of it, averages between 60in and 100in a year.

North of the Amazon are the Guiana Highlands which are partly forested. The Brazilian Highlands lie between the Amazon and the La Plata basin in the south and form a tableland of between 1,000ft and 3,000ft high which in most parts dips sharply down to the sea. This Great Escarpment peters out near Porto Alegre, capital of the state of Rio Grande do Sul, and from here to the south the country opens out into a fertile plain where Aberdeen Angus, Shorthorn and Hereford cattle graze in lush pastures.

Brazil's known mineral resources are vast and include manganese ore, copper, aluminium, zinc, lead, tin and nickel. Gold and diamond prospecting is carried out in several areas of the country. The gold-mine of Morro Velho, near Belo Horizonte, is the deepest mine in the Americas and goes down 8,501ft. It was opened by a British company in 1834 but was sold to Brazil in 1959. Brazil's reserves of iron ore have been estimated to be between 70 and 100 billion tons, or enough to supply the whole world for 150 years at present consumption levels. It is confidently expected that new and probably large sources of mineral wealth will be found in the Amazon region as pioneers and roads advance deeper into hitherto unknown areas.

CLIMATE

Brazil's climate is moderate in spite of the fact that most of the country is within the tropical zone. The average annual temperature decreases from north to south. In the Amazon basin it is about 81° F (27° C), whereas between Recife and Rio de Janeiro the mean temperature is from 74° to 80° along the coast. In the Highlands it is from 64° to 70°, while between Rio de Janeiro and Brazil's southern frontier the mean temperature is from 62° to 66°. Frosts occur in the more southerly areas of the country and often cause havoc among coffee plantations in the state of Paraná, for instance. Humidity is high, especially along the coast. Generally speaking, most areas of Brazil suffer from neither too much nor too little rainfall; but an exception is the North-east, where a state of disaster is often declared as a result of prolonged droughts or floods.

FLORA AND FAUNA

Brazil is an immense treasure-chest of flora and fauna and it is claimed that in the Amazon region, for instance, there can be found as many as 3,000 different species of plants per square mile. There exists a wealth of hard and soft woods including the Paraná pine, mahogany and various kinds of jacaranda. Brazil is said to have gained its name from the *pau Brasil*, a tree yielding a red dye which was much sought after immediately following the arrival of the first Portuguese discoverers in 1500. Some concern is felt in Brazil about the rapid rate at which its forest reserves are being felled, and views have been expressed both in and outside the country that the cutting down of large areas of Amazon forest will deprive the world of a great deal of oxygen. Fortunately, in the past few years the Brazilian authorities have introduced measures aimed at curbing deforestation and increasing afforestation. Action has also been taken to prohibit the export of certain skins (of otters, for example) to prevent fauna from becoming extinct as a result of sustained hunting for commercial purposes. Brazil has no big game as such, but in the country can be found wild boar, deer, jaguar, ocelot, tapir, ant-eater and capybara. There are enormous varieties of insects, beetles and butterflies as well as exotic flowers and plants, such as orchids, to make up a botanist's paradise. Certain rivers abound with the ferocious piranha fish which are attracted to their victims, humans included, by the smell of blood. In a matter of minutes they can reduce a steer to nothing but bones. Rivers such as the Araguaia yield the delicious pirarucú fish, called *piroska* by the Karajá Indians, who appreciate them greatly. These fish can easily weigh 150lb (142kg) each. When dried, the tongue of the pirarucú is as hard as steel and becomes the rasp on which the Maué Indians are said to grate the guaraná berry. Another large and very tasty fish is the *tucunaré*, sometimes called the salmon of the Amazon. Many types of salt-water fish are caught off Brazil's coasts and its northern and north-eastern waters yield the bulk of the shrimp and lobster catch.

Brazilian plant life furnishes huge resources for the herbalist since there are hundreds of trees, shrubs and herbs with accredited medicinal properties. The basic material can be bought in markets or in herb shops. The most popular remedy for liver complaints is an infusion made from leaves of the *boldo* plant. It is claimed that tumours, boils and carbuncles can be cured by the application of a particular orchid of the Catasetum genera which has been skinned and mashed. The cashew is credited with the following impressive list of properties: the fruit is antisyphilitic; the nut is an aphrodisiac, good for the memory and a caustic against ulcers; the skin of the nut is corrosive and can be used effectively on warts and wrinkles; the gum from the tree is obnoxious to insects and is recommended for bookbinding; the juice from the bark of the tree gives indelible ink; the bark is a tonic, astringent and antidiabetic; and the tree itself is planted in the North-east of Brazil to provide shade for coffee-trees. What more could one ask from one single product of nature?

RACIAL ORIGINS

When Brazil was discovered by the Portuguese in 1500, its population consisted of Indians whose number at that time has been variously estimated at between 2 and 4 million. The first colonisers were Portuguese; but later there was an influx to Brazil of African slaves and immigrants of many nationalities, with the result that the country became probably the biggest racial melting-pot in the world. During the early colonial days there was widespread miscegenation between Negroes and whites, Negroes and Indians, and Indians and whites which produced progeny classified as mulattos, *cafusos*, *caboclos*, mamelucos and mestizos. Intermarriage between these types over subsequent years has produced many individuals whose racial origins are as bewildering as their colour is in many cases difficult to define. With the evolution of the country and the growth of its population, however, the old colonial colour and racial classifications fell out of use. Whatever their racial origins, the people of the country have become welded into a nation of Brazilians who think like Brazilians regardless of colour or creed. Brazil's ability to absorb people of all kinds into a general community is truly remarkable.

Throughout the country there is a lack of colour or racial consciousness and there are laws to prevent discrimination on these grounds. The Brazilian sociologist Dr Gilberto Freyre has drawn attention to the growing tendency on the part of the non-white population, whatever their shades of colour, merely to refer to themselves as *moreno*, which means dark or brunette. Difference of colour is not an issue, as is shown by the fact that there was no provision in the most recent official census papers for members of the population to register their colour.

B

Brazil's present-day population of Negroes is approximately 15 per cent of that of the whole country, whereas the mixed population is around 25 per cent. Although most Brazilians are descended from Portuguese stock, there are many other racial influences to be seen. Strong German communities established themselves in the southern states of Rio Grande do Sul, Santa Catarina and Paraná. About 600,000 Japanese have settled in Brazil and most of the intensive market gardening, principally around the city of São Paulo, is carried out by them. There are large communities of Hungarians, Italians, Lebanese, Poles, Russians, Spaniards and Syrians, settled mainly in São Paulo and in the southern states. Chinese were brought to Brazil in the early nineteenth century to start tea planting under arrangements made by the then Brazilian Minister for External Affairs, but it was an experiment on a small scale. About eighty miles from São Paulo, near Campinas, there is a town called Americana which was founded by Confederate families who left the USA to start new lives in Brazil after the defeat of their cause in the American Civil War. It is calculated that 2,070 of these immigrants, who were from the states of Alabama, Florida, Louisiana, Mississippi, South Carolina, Tennessee, Texas and Virginia, arrived in Brazil between 1866 and 1867. They did not all settle in the same part of Brazil: 800 established themselves in the state of São Paulo; 400 in Espírito Santo; 200 in Paraná; 200 in Rio de Janeiro; 200 in Pará; 100 in Minas Gerais; 100 in Bahia; and 70 in Pernambuco. Colonel William Norris and his group were the first to arrive in Americana in 1866, bringing agricultural implements with them. They quickly started growing cotton, which proved successful, and were the first people to cultivate water-melons in their area.

There has also been a fair number of immigrants to Brazil from the British Isles, starting with Scottish workmen who were employed in 1637 on sugar estates near Recife during the Dutch occupation of the north-east from 1630 to 1649. An English engineer named William Bragg was responsible for building the first Brazilian railway, linking Rio and Petropolis, which started operating in 1854; British engineers were concerned with the building of other railways in Brazil as well as the provision of tram services, hydroelectric plant and telegraph communications. British agricultural communities were also established from 1860 onwards in the state of Paraná. In 1827 Emperor Pedro I of Brazil sent Colonel William Cotter, an Irishman, to Cork for the purpose of recruiting Irishmen to fight in the Brazilian army in Brazil's war with Argentina. Colonel Cotter managed to recruit 2,686 Irishmen, about 2,000 of whom were subsequently enrolled in the 2nd and 3rd Battalions of Grenadiers and the 28th Battalion of Light Infantry quartered in Rio de Janeiro. The Irish created several disturbances, however, and arguments about their contracts, pay and corporal punishment inflicted on them finally led them to mutiny. After a good deal of trouble the emperor permitted the majority of the Irish to leave the Brazilian army and to be established in agricultural communities in the states of Rio Grande do Sul, Santa Catarina, Paraná, São Paulo and Espírito Santo. Another agricultural community of 101 Irish families was established in 1828 at Taperoá in the state of Bahia, but there appears to be no trace of their descendants in that district today.

There are so many types in Brazil, ranging from the leather-suited *vaqueiros* or cowboys of the North-east to their gaucho counterparts in the South who wear *bombachas* or baggy riding trousers, that it is virtually impossible to define a representative Brazilian. Each region has its own type of inhabitant, music, food and accent; but the remarkable fact is that all the people speak the same language and think as Brazilians, even though they live scattered over an immense area and in some cases as far as 2,000 miles from each other.

POPULATION

Brazil's demographic growth was slow until the early nineteenth century, but since then it has increased at an astonishing rate. In 1800, three centuries after the country was discovered, it was probably no more than 3 million. From 1800 to 1920 it increased ten times. The census of 1900 showed the population as 17,438,434 and that of 1940 as 41,236,315; the preliminary figures for the most recent census taken in September 1970 give the population as 94,508,554. This is a little under one and three-quarter times larger than the population of the UK and less than half of that of the USA. Between 1960 and 1970 the Brazilian population increased by about 23½ million; and this growth-rate has led experts to estimate that Brazilians will number 200 million by the end of this century, a figure roughly equivalent to the present population of the whole of South America. An even more telling estimate is that by the year 2000 the population of the city of São Paulo alone will be nearly as large as was the population of the whole of Brazil in 1900.

A growth-rate of 3·5 per cent (according to the 1970 census, this figure was reduced to 2·7 per cent for the period 1960–70) and a birth-rate of over 40 per 1,000 coupled with a reduction in infant mortality, have resulted in over half of Brazil's population being under the age of 21. It has been estimated that the number of Brazilians under the age of 19 increased from 45·74 per cent in 1872 to 52·86 per cent in 1960 and this high proportion of young people has continued, especially as an average Brazilian family numbers 7 children.

Official figures show that 3,648,382 immigrants were admitted to Brazil for the period from 1820 to 1920. Between 1884 and 1939 the number was 4,158,717. The Italians contributed 1,412,263 immigrants, the Portuguese 1,204,394 and the Spaniards 581,718; and there were immigrants of other nationalities. It must be remembered, however, that many of these immigrants came to speculate rather than to spend the rest of their lives in Brazil; and indeed many returned to their home countries after what was often a profitable stay. At the beginning of the present century there was an influx of about 100,000 immigrants to Brazil per year, but this rate was not maintained. From about 80,000 in 1952 and close to 50,000 in 1958, there was a drop to 23,859 immigrant arrivals in 1963. This reduction was due not only to the migration of labour towards other countries such as Australia, Canada and the USA, but also to difficulties in the Latin American labour markets along with foreign exchange and political considerations.

The density of Brazil's population is most uneven and in Rio de Janeiro, for instance, it is roughly eighty times higher than it is in the state of Amazonas. For centuries over three-quarters of the population has been concentrated within 100 miles of the coast, in a narrow belt which has always been the area of industrial and agricultural development. This traditional pattern is starting to change, however, as people move on newly built roads into hitherto undeveloped parts of the interior where young cities, industries and commercial enterprises are beginning to blossom. Outstanding examples of this advance into the hinterland are the cities of Brasilia and Goiânia in the very heart of the country; the Belém–Brasilia road; and the bold enterprise of the transamazonian highway, which is being driven from east to west through tracts of unexplored jungle, to establish a road link between the Atlantic and the Pacific over a distance about the same as that from Boston to San Francisco.

LANGUAGE

The official language of the country is Portuguese, but Brazilian Portuguese is different in several ways—not only from the point of view of accent—from the Portuguese spoken in Portugal. As examples, communication by telephone in Portugal is established by saying *está*; but in Brazil the word used is *alô*. The phrase *pois não* in Portugal is a negative, whereas in Brazil it is used as a gambit in conversation to mean 'yes, of course'. There are several differences of this nature which can cause confusion. The number 6 in Portugal is *seis*; but in Brazil it is often referred to, especially where telephone numbers are concerned, as *meia dúzia* or half a dozen. In Portugal a girl is called a *rapariga*; but in Brazil the word has different connotations which are hardly flattering and its use is best avoided.

Even within Brazil there is quite a regional variation of accent between people from different states. The gaucho, or native of Rio Grande do Sul, usually has a sprinkling of Spanish in his language due to his state's proximity to Uruguay and Argentina. The Portuguese of the Paulista, native of São Paulo, has been influenced by a large number of Italian immigrants, but it is probably the easiest dialect for a foreigner to understand since it is more clearly enunciated than that spoken by, for example, the Carioca or inhabitant of the city of Rio de Janeiro.

Portuguese is a Latin language and it has been described by some as Latin with different endings. It is said to be an easy language to learn, but many express their doubts on this point. Certainly it is an expressive language, for one frequently finds that six or more English words are in many cases necessary to translate one Portuguese word. A good example is *saudade*, a word used constantly in Brazil: it means a combination of yearning and nostalgia and more than that, in a way which cannot readily be expressed in English. Another word is *jeitinho*: when someone tells you that something is impossible, then you ask him whether it would not be possible to arrange whatever it is by a *jeitinho* (the diminutive of *jeito*). It is not quite correct to translate this as 'fix' or 'arrange'. It is something a little more than that, and the extra meaning is untranslatable because personal relationship is involved as well as a mere word.

There has been some Anglo-Saxon influence on Brazilian Portuguese especially where sport is concerned. When a player of *futebol* makes a *chute* at the *gol* he kicks the *bola* with his *chuteira* (football boot) and hopes that the *golkeeper* or *goleiro* does not stop it. A boxer lays low his opponent by a *nocaute*. A drinker of Scotch selects his favourite brand of *uisque*. An unusual expression peculiar to the state of Mato Grosso is 'all Smith' (*tudo Smith*), which is used to mean 'very good'. The 'Smith' is pronounced 'Shmeety' and derives from the Smith and Wesson revolver, which has always enjoyed the reputation in that land of the six-gun of being the finest revolver available, having pride of place above all others including the Colt. Thus

'Smith' came to mean first-class in Mato Grosso. The spelling
of foreign dishes on menus in some Brazilian restaurants can
baffle the clientele, Brazilians and foreigners alike. A Brazilian
ambassador, his curiosity aroused by having read that *aristu*
was a recommended dish of the day, found that it was in fact
Irish stew.

There are many slang terms in Brazil which a newcomer
can learn only with time. Thus when you ask a Brazilian how
his affairs are going he may reply that things are 'all blue'
(*tudo azul*), meaning that everything is fine. He may tell you
that he has completed a 'Chinese deal' (*negocio da China*), an
excellent business; but if he says that he bought a 'pineapple'
(*abacaxi*), then the deal was a bad one from his point of view.
The Brazilian usually accompanies his conversation with
expressive gestures of the hands, and indeed many of these
gestures can adequately convey meaning without the use of
words. If he takes the lobe of his right ear between his thumb
and forefinger, he is expressing keen appreciation of whatever
is being discussed. If he pulls down his right lower eyelid with
his forefinger, then he is warning you to be careful. A study of
these expressive gestures and gesticulations is a fascinating one,
but to acquire the technique of executing them correctly
requires both time and experience.

It is not difficult for the foreigner to gain a working knowledge of the Brazilian language in a reasonably short time.
Brazilians are most appreciative of any efforts, however
rudimentary they may be, which a foreigner makes to speak to
them in their own tongue; and he should not be disconcerted
or deterred if he later hears them lapse into near-perfect
English.

NATIONAL CHARACTERISTICS

The average Brazilian is good-natured and possessed of an
excellent sense of humour which enables him to crack a joke
even when things go wrong. Brazilian wit is often astringent
without being unkind, and amusing without giving offence.

A typical example of Brazilian wit occurred when the British aircraft carrier *Ark Royal* put in at Rio during World War II. It was well known in Brazil that the Germans had claimed on many occasions to have sunk this ship, and Brazilian wags were determined to make the most of the *Ark Royal's* safe arrival at Rio. The following day the local newspapers, including those not entirely favourable to the Allied cause at that time, came out with banner headlines announcing the arrival of 'the biggest submarine in the world'. No one could really take offence. The Brazilians tell many jokes about the Portuguese which show them in something of an unfavourable light, but admit with relish that the Portuguese tell similar jokes about the Brazilians. Many Brazilians are equally incorrigible when it comes to making up stories about situations in their own country. During 1970 the habit came in of sticking patriotic slogans on the rear windows of cars, and possibly the most popular one read: 'Brazil—love it or leave it.' The wags soon had a follow-up reply circulating round Rio: 'Last one to leave turns the lights out.'

A characteristic of Brazilians is their tremendous love of their country, however much they may decry it at times. Whatever state they come from, they really love Brazil and with good reason. In bygone days many Brazilians tended to apologise to foreigners for national shortcomings, but this attitude is beginning to change as Brazil takes rapid strides on the road to becoming a major power. Its increasing prosperity and importance have reduced any sense of inferiority which Brazilians may have felt in the past towards more developed countries, and there is justification for this change of attitude. Brazil has first-class technicians, architects, doctors, dentists, lawyers, schoolteachers, university professors, government employees and other excellent representatives in every walk of life. Brazil is even suffering from the brain drain as far as its scientists are concerned.

Brazilians are not militarists although military service is obligatory and they have gone to war when the occasion has demanded it. For instance, a Brazilian expeditionary force fought well in Italy during World War II. The Brazilian armed forces enjoy prestige within the country and by tradition are the guardians of the institutions which they defend when necessary. They also patrol immense distances of frontier and carry out many civic duties.

Brazilians are generally considered to dislike violence. This is probably true as regards mob violence but does not mean that they are incapable of individual acts of violence. On the contrary, when passions are aroused there is often bloodshed.

One of the most appealing characteristics of Brazilians is their great and touching love for children, whom they tend to spoil. No one accustomed to the rather sterner Anglo-Saxon methods of handling children could fail to be impressed by the patience and tolerance with which the average Brazilian father treats his offspring on a Sunday family outing.

Family feeling is strong and the younger generation usually treat parents and grandparents, aunts, uncles and in-laws with affection and respect. The average Brazilian wife looks after her husband tenderly but likes to remain in the background, giving the appearance of being something of a subdued alter ego. But this does not mean that Brazilian women are entirely submissive and have no interests outside the home. Many of them do sterling if often unsung work in charitable and other organisations. The power which they exercise in the land is used in such a discreet and amiable manner that their husbands in no way feel that their traditional position as the dominant male and breadwinning head of the family is being questioned or undermined.

A large number of Brazilian women work in the professions and there are, for instance, capable and respected female lawyers, doctors, journalists, members of Congress and newspaper owners. Brazil can even boast a woman football referee.

Brazilian men work hard but know how to enjoy their leisure. There is an old saying in Brazil that São Paulo is the place for work and Rio the place for play. Nevertheless, Cariocas or inhabitants of Rio put in surprisingly long hours of work in spite of the enervating climate and the almost irresistible beach and other attractions easily visible from office windows.

Impetuous, kind, generous, amusing, sometimes flippant, often unpunctual, a good friend, the Brazilian is all of these. In a curious way the greatest favour you can do him is to let him do you a favour. In some inexplicable fashion this establishes a bond between the two of you, and if you can establish a bond with a Brazilian then he will usually prove to be a life-long friend.

Brazilians, especially the country people, are superstitious and follow a bewildering number of customs to avoid bad luck or disaster. It is said that Santos Dumont, the Brazilian pioneer of aviation, even went so far as to have the stairs in his house constructed in such a way that it was physically impossible to start climbing them with the left foot: he believed it essential to start with the right foot, otherwise all kinds of disaster might ensue. Country people never tread in anyone's shadow, nor do they look over their shoulders when walking alone in the wilds: they believe that to do so brings an eerie feeling of spookiness and that a jaguar will follow up behind and attack.

In the state of São Paulo it is considered bad luck to kill a snake inside the house.

A broom, symbol of witches, is thought to be possessed of strong powers and must always be left in an upright position unless the owner wishes to get rid of guests who have overstayed their welcome, when it should be placed upside down behind the door.

A woman in love, anxious to make a man return her affections when he gives no sign of doing so, will prepare a drink of tea, coffee or chocolate strained through her petticoat when it is damp with perspiration, and get the man to swallow this. He is then supposed to become irresistibly attracted to her.

Wax matches are not used, because they are considered to be reminiscent of small candles used at funerals and therefore unlucky. A factory which started producing wax matches in Brazil had to go into liquidation within a short time.

Hunters in the jungle are nearly always doomed if they have

the bad luck to run across *Mapinguari*, a huge man-monster covered with red hair. Men's heads are his favourite form of food. He makes his victims faint merely by blowing his fetid breath on them and then tears them to pieces with razor-sharp claws. He is said to be impervious to bullets unless shot exactly through the navel.

There is a superstition in the cattlelands about a phantom cowboy who appears on ranches when the round-up and branding are taking place. No one knows where he comes from or where he lives. He rides an apparently decrepit horse but is able to gallop dozens of miles in a matter of minutes; he can round up an entire herd in an hour or two. Powerful bulls remain motionless at his merest word or gesture. Women pine for him. The mysterious cowpuncher refuses their advances but defeats his competitors in every other way, including eating and drinking. After collecting his pay he vanishes, only to reappear shortly afterwards on another ranch as much as 150 miles away, where he goes through the same routine.

In the state of Rio Grande do Sul there is the story of the little Negro herder who, as the slave of a rich and evil farmer, looked after a herd of dun horses. One day he lost them and, on the orders of his owner, was beaten up and thrown, still bleeding, into an ants' nest where he died. Superstition has it that the boy can often be heard riding across the pastures at the head of his troop of horses.

One of the best known characters of Brazilian legend and superstition is a mischievous gnome or hobgoblin called Sacy-Pereré. If descriptions of him are to be believed, he has one eye, one leg, is the size of a small boy, wears a red cap and has an unlit pipe in his mouth. These distinctive characteristics make it easy to identify him. He is said to stop passers-by and to ask for a light, but they should be careful because he is a troublemaker and capable of almost any devilry. When country people find that their horses are jaded in the mornings and have their manes all knotted, they blame it on Sacy-Pereré; they say that he enjoys borrowing horses for night-rides and has to knot their manes in order to hang on.

Many Brazilian legends, customs and superstitions are a curious mixture derived from the influence of European culture brought by the colonists; religious teaching; African culture brought over with the slaves; and Brazilian Indian beliefs. Some Indian legends have survived in their purest form, however, and one of the most charming is that which explains the discovery of guaraná by the Maué Indians. The berries of the guaraná plant (*Paullinia cupana*) contain guaranine, an alkaloid nerve-stimulant said to be good for the health. It is used in the manufacture of a soft drink called guaraná, which is widely drunk in Brazil and is also now being exported.

According to the legend, many years ago a husband and wife among the Maué Indians had a son who, as he grew up, brought great prosperity to the tribe. They always found plenty to eat and, if any of them became ill, their aches and ailments were cured by the young boy who was treated by the whole tribe with the greatest respect and affection. This period of general happiness was brought to an end, however, by Jaruparí, an evil spirit, who became jealous of the young Maué. One day when the boy was climbing a tree to pick some fruit, Jaruparí turned himself into a snake and attacked him.

The Indians found the boy lying dead on the ground beneath the tree, with his eyes wide open and serene. As, overcome with grief, they stood weeping round the dead boy, a ray suddenly appeared in the sky and touched the ground near them. The silence which followed was broken by the mother of the dead boy who announced that their god Tupá had come down to earth to console the tribe. His orders were, she said, that the eyes of the dead boy should be plucked out and planted in the ground, because from them there would grow a wonderful plant which would not only feed the Maué Indians but would cure their sicknesses as well.

The eyes of the boy were plucked out and planted in a small earth plot which was watered by the tears of the Indians. The oldest members of the tribe remained on watch to see what would happen. A plant which soon began to grow in the plot was looked after tenderly by the tribe. Not long afterwards berries appeared on the plant and they looked just like the eyes of a child. This plant was the guaraná and its berries were the secret food and remedy given by the god Tupá to the Maué Indians.

THE INDIANS

At the time of its discovery Brazil was populated by four main linguistic groups of Indians, the Tupi-Guarani, Gê, Arawakan and Carib. The Tupi were widespread in the coastal areas and in the Xingú and Tapajós regions. The Gê were forced back from the coast by the Tupi and settled on Brazil's eastern plateau, while the Arawakans lived in the North-east and the Caribs in the Guianas, Venezuela and neighbouring areas. Continual intertribal warfare resulted in the elimination or assimilation of some groups. Tupi-Guarani was the *lingua geral* and up to the end of the eighteenth century about 80 per cent of the Brazilian population spoke it.

When the Portuguese discoverers of Brazil arrived at Porto Seguro in 1500, they were met by coastal Indians who received these strange visitors to their shores in a spirit of innocence and curiosity. The welcoming attitude of the Indians changed later to one of resistance, when it became clear to them that the Europeans had come to stay and to exploit whatever riches this new territory might provide. The Indians fought doggedly to defend their traditional hunting grounds but they were either killed, enslaved or driven inland. Some tribes became allies of the Europeans while others, especially the Guarani, accepted the tutelage of the Jesuits and allowed themselves to be herded into missions where the surroundings and régime were entirely different from their natural life and habitat. A few tribes fought on. The Guaikurú or Horsemen Indians of Mato Grosso, for example, were bitter adversaries of the colonisers until 1791, when they were finally persuaded to sign a treaty of peace and friendship with the Portuguese. Contact with the Xavantes, a much feared tribe, was achieved only just over twenty years ago. The Cintas Largas have not yet responded fully to friendly overtures which have been made to them for more than two years. Only in 1973 did the Vilas Boas brothers Orlando and Claudio, well known for their work among the Indians in the Xingú National Park, at last make contact with the Kranhakarore 'giant' Indians after patient efforts lasting nearly five years. The 'giants' were found to be tall and well made but not of the gigantic stature attributed to them by other Indians. Further groups of Indians will no doubt be discovered when unexplored areas of the country are developed.

It was not until the early days of Brazilian independence that a more merciful policy towards Brazilian Indians was introduced by the statesman José Bonifácio, who called for justice and kindliness in dealing with them and the establishment of trading relations. Previously the Indian had been treated as nothing but a brutish savage. In 1910 the Indian Protection Service (SPI) was created and the famous Marshal (then General) Candido Mariano da Silva Rondon, himself part Indian, was put in charge of it. His motto, 'Die if necessary, never kill', was the splendid philosophy and policy of the service he commanded and he and his subordinates carried out magnificent work. The principal óbjectives laid down for the SPI were to protect, support and help the life, liberty and property of the Indians; to protect him from persecution, exploitation, oppression and misery; to educate and instruct him; to guarantee his possession of land; to respect and to cause to be respected within reasonable moral bounds the organisation, independence, ways and customs of tribes; to pacify tribes by removing the reasons for hostility; to protect and defend the indigenous family; to give moral and civic instruction in order to strengthen the Indian's qualities and traditions and at the same time to make him understand the part he has to play both in the tribe and in the common home country; to look after the well-being of the Indian by improving his living conditions; to develop his relations with 'civilised ones' in a sense of respect, help and friendship; to increase effective means of helping and protecting him; and to make a study of the Indian in ethnological, anthro-

pological, biographic, artistic, industrial, linguistic and archae-
ological fields.

After Rondon's death the Brazilian SPI began to go downhill.
In September 1967 an official inquiry was made into its activities,
resulting in shattering disclosures about embezzlement of
official funds, the taking over of Indians' land, enslavement of
Indians and methods used for their extermination. Many SPI
officials were suspended or dismissed. The inquiry aroused
world interest and Brazil was accused of practising a policy of
genocide towards its indigenous population, an accusation
refuted by the Brazilian government. Most serious observers
of the problem agreed that the government had never been
guilty of such a policy, although at the same time it was generally
recognised that official action to protect Indians from the
activities of rubber-tappers, prospectors and land companies
was often woefully inadequate or non-existent. In many cases
Indian land represented a desirable source of mineral and
agricultural wealth to settlers who were determined to acquire
it even if the rightful owners had to be killed or pushed out of
it in the process of spoliation. A particularly revolting example
of cruelty towards Indians was given by land colonisers who
left 'presents' of sugar laced with arsenic on the banks of the
river Arinos for the *Beiços de pau* or 'wood-lipped' Indians. But
this was an action by unscrupulous individuals, not by the
government.

As a result of the inquiry, the SPI was dissolved and a new
organisation called the National Indian Foundation (FUNAI)
was created by Law No 5,371 of 5 December 1967 to take its
place. This absorbed the National Council for the Protection
of the Indian, the SPI and the Xingú National Park. The basic
aims of FUNAI are to promote the economic development of
integrated tribes, to speed the acculturation of others, to watch
over missionary work among the Indians, to pacify tribes in
conflict with white men, to look after the Indians' health, and
to police Indian lands by using the Indians themselves for this
work.

The efforts of FUNAI have been hampered by a lack of

funds and trained personnel. Many experts feel that Indian affairs should be handled by a department directly subordinate to the President, rather than to the Ministry of the Interior as FUNAI is at present.

There are three basic schools of thought about the treatment of Brazilian Indians. The first is the so-called 'zoological park' school, which maintains that Indians should be kept in reservations entirely isolated from contact with civilisation. The second school advocates the quickest possible integration of the Indian into civilised society in order that he shall be able to take his place in national life, alongside other Brazilian citizens, as a person with a trade. The third school, which is probably the most logical one, believes that the Indian should not be denied the benefits of civilisation, if he wishes to learn about them, but that the process of integration should be carried out at a gentle pace. This was in fact the policy accepted by Brazil under Convention 107, which was adopted in Geneva on 26 June 1957 at the fortieth session of the General Conference of the International Labour Organisation and promulgated in Brazil by Decree No 58,824 of 14 July 1966.

Under Article 2 of this Convention, the Brazilian authorities undertook to promote the progressive integration of Brazilian

———

A girl sieves coffee at a drying yard or *terreiro*. There is quite an art in throwing up the coffee and catching it intact again in the sieve

View of a coffee *fazenda* or farm in the state of São Paulo. New and quicker-producing varieties of coffee-trees have taken the place of many old plantations

Indians in order that they should benefit on terms of equality from the rights and opportunities which national legislation grants to other elements of the population. Brazil was also obliged under the terms of the Convention to promote the social, economic and cultural development of its Indians as well as the improvement of their standards of living, and to create possibilities for national integration with the exclusion of any measure aimed at the 'artificial assimilation' of the Indian population. The Brazilian authorities interpreted 'natural assimilation' to be that sought voluntarily by the Indian when he abandons of his own free will the tribal community and adopts and accepts all the customs and institutions of civilised life. It is the declared policy of FUNAI to resist, under the terms of Brazil's international undertaking, any 'forced assimilation' which imposes on the Indians against their will the customs, beliefs and institutions of civilised society; and in any case item 4 of Article 2 of Convention 107 precludes the use of any force or coercion for the purpose of integration.

The coveting of Indian lands is and always has been a major problem in so far as the protection of Indians is concerned, and the problem becomes greater now that the interior of the country is being developed. Several official parks and reservations have

———

A view of the transamazonian road which is being hacked through the jungle of North Brazil. A large stretch of the road was inaugurated by Brazil's president in September 1972

Agricultural settlements established in the middle of the jungle beside the transamazonian highway. Understandably, buildings are constructed mainly of wood been established but already those of the Xingú and Tumucu-maque are threatened by new roads which will cut through them. Since the discovery of Brazil there have been clashes between Indians and encroaching settlers who destroy the flora and fauna on which the Indians depend for their existence. It will be a bleak outlook for the Indians unless the Brazilian authorities can grant and guarantee adequate reservations for their use.

The provision of adequate prophylactic medical attention is also vital since Indians have no resistance to diseases brought by civilisation: epidemics of measles or influenza in a tribe can be as lethal as bullets. Much dedicated medical work among Brazilian Indians has been and continues to be done, especially by the Brazilian air force, but the scope of the effort is still small in relation to a big problem. Tribes with the best health record are those kept in the Xingú National Park under the care of Claudio and Orlando Vilas Boas, two brothers who have dedicated their lives to the Indians and who are undoubtedly the greatest experts on the subject.

It is estimated that, from about 4 million Indians living in Brazil at the time of its being discovered in 1500, there are between 70,000 and 120,000 tribal Indians still living today as their survivors. Great warrior tribes like the Kayapó, Karajá, Kadiweu, Bororo and Xavantes survive, though they are sadly depleted in numbers. They still call themselves nations, not tribes, and are proud of their history and their cultural heritage. Despite the influence of missionaries and other *civilizados* over the years, they still seem to prefer their tribal way of life, though many of them have adopted civilised clothes. The Bororo Indians, who have been in touch with civilisation for well over two centuries, claim that in all that time there has been only one case of religious conversion: that of a Roman Catholic priest who was converted to the Bororo religion.

The future of the Indians appears problematical in a rapidly developing country like Brazil where new roads are being built, forests cut down, mineral resources exploited, and where the occupation by Indians of large areas of land may become increasingly inconvenient as far as the country's economic interests are concerned. If they tackle the problem with sympathy and sincerity, the Brazilian authorities have a great opportunity to show the world that an indigenous population can be preserved with grace and dignity, and that the Indian can be given an opportunity to play an honourable and useful role in his own country.

RELIGION

Brazil is acknowledged to be the largest Roman Catholic country in the world. The official Brazilian figures for 1969 show that there were 34,172 Roman Catholic places of worship in the country and 7,606 priests, a small number in relation to the vast size of the country. Something like a little more than 40 per cent of the priests in Brazil are foreign and nearly 1,000 of them are Dutch. Others are from Belgium, Germany, Italy, Poland, Spain and the USA. There are also Irish nuns and Canadian priests serving in Brazil.

Freedom of worship is guaranteed to all in Brazil and there are many Protestants as well as numerous devotees of Umbanda, Macumba and such cults of African origin which were brought to Brazil, in their original form, by the slaves. Macumba, which has been described as Brazilian voodoo, exerts powerful influences and should not be dismissed as meaningless mumbo-jumbo. Sessions are said to be best on Friday evenings because the spirits are then freer. Bottles and burning candles grouped on the pavement at the corner of a street-crossing mean that a Macumba service is taking place in favour of something or somebody or against something or somebody. These indications, which are called *despachos*, are not necessarily near the place (*terreiro*) where the service is being held. Newcomers to Macumba may be surprised to find that St George or Ogum occupies an all-important place in the ceremonies.

A cult which is gaining an increasing number of adherents, even from the wealthier classes, is that of Iemanjá, goddess of the sea and of those who take their living from the sea. She is known under a dozen other titles including Queen of the Sea, Mermaid of the Sea and Dona Janaína. The fan and the sword are her insignia and her sacred foods are pigeons, maize, cocks and emasculated goats. Her ritual colours are red, dark blue and rose. Jealous, vindictive and cruel, Iemanjá takes lovers to the bottom of the sea and does not even return their bodies. Small wonder, therefore, that she has to be propitiated. On New Year's Eve the beaches of Rio are crowded with her followers who go through various rituals before throwing flowers and other offerings, including jewellery even, into the sea to propitiate Iemanjá. Model boats containing presents are tenderly entrusted to the waters and dispatched out to sea in the hope that they will be accepted by Dona Janaína. Devotees may themselves go out in boats and throw their offerings over the side, then wait anxiously to see the result. If the offerings are carried out to sea, then Iemanjá has been pleased to accept them; but if the tide washes them back on to the beach, Iemanjá is angry and the year is going to be a bad one.

In a Roman Catholic country like Brazil, saints have always been popular and St Antony of Padua probably enjoys the greatest following of them all. Girls pray to him to find a husband for them and rarely do their prayers go unanswered. Whenever an object is mislaid, then a prayer to St Antony will usually soon cause it to be found. The pommel on a Brazilian-type saddle is called a *santantonio* and very comforting it can be to the rider at difficult moments.

St Antony, highly regarded for his effectiveness in military affairs, was always considered by the people of Bahia to be their protector; and in 1598 he was made town patron. In 1705 the townspeople made a request to the governor that, as an expression of their gratitude to the saint for his favours and protection, St Antony should be promoted to be a captain of the fortress of Barra and rewarded with a captain's pay. This request was granted by the governor and later confirmed by Dom João V in a royal letter. The image of St Antony was thereafter decorated with a military dagger, hat, epaulettes and sword. St Antony was promoted to major and later to lieutenant-colonel. His salary continued to be paid, even after Brazil became a republic, until 1911 when the then Minister of War stopped it. St Antony was greatly venerated in other parts of Brazil as well: his image enjoyed the rank of soldier in the states of Paraíba and Espírito Santo, of lieutenant in Recife, captain in Goiás, captain of cavalry in Vila Rica, captain in the state of Rio Grande do Norte, lieutenant-colonel in Rio de Janeiro and colonel in São Paulo. He was also granted the status of alderman in Iguarucú, Pernambuco.

A curious incident occurred in the state of Bahia during the nineteenth century at a farm called Queimadas belonging to a very devout lady who, in 1842, built a chapel there dedicated to St Antony. The lady gave a large number of slaves and a great deal of her land to her patron saint. After a party one night, a slave belonging to St Antony killed someone inside the chapel. The criminal escaped and no further trace of him was found. Under Article 28 of the Criminal Code of the Empire, the owner of a slave was held responsible in those days for any crime committed by the slave if he did not hand him over to justice. A legal case was brought against St Antony as the owner of the runaway slave and the saint's image, trussed up with ropes, was placed on a mule and carried off to prison in the old village of Agua Fria where justice was known to be implacable. The image of St Antony was taken to court and placed on the bench of the accused. He was found guilty and condemned to lose his possessions. All the lands and slaves belonging to St Antony were taken over by a local farmer. Even as late as 1930 there was a case running in the courts of Bahia connected with this takeover of land from the chapel of St Antony of Queimadas.

Many priests made their mark on Brazilian history, especially during colonial and empire days, as a result of their selfless devotion to the spiritual cause they served. Padre Antonio Vieira made a name for himself in the 1650s through his thunderings from the pulpit about the evils of slavery. Jesuits worked tirelessly and heroically among the Indians until their Order was expelled from Brazil. But on the whole the Church adopted a passive attitude towards the political life of the country and was submissive to the interests and actions of the State. During the last decade, however, the Roman Catholic Church in Brazil has adopted a much more positive and sometimes aggressive stance in regard to social problems within the country, and this has on occasion led to friction between Church and State. Serious rifts have been avoided by the desire of those concerned to patch up quarrels. There are alleged to be differences within the Church itself between the so-called 'conservative' and 'progressive' groups, both of them considered to be minorities among the large bulk of nearly 240 Brazilian bishops, the majority of whom are not yet committed to either group. Probably the best-known 'progressive' priest is Dom Helder Camara, Archbishop of Olinda and Recife, who has carried out vociferous campaigns, both at home and abroad, for the improvement of social conditions in the country. This volatile archbishop has incurred a certain amount of unpopularity among his countrymen by criticising Brazil during his travels abroad, but he can nevertheless count on the continued support of a group of devoted followers.

Members of the 'progressive' wing of the Brazilian Church are opposed to the government's policy of economic development at all costs and maintain that the improvement of social conditions is a matter of greater immediate priority.

In May 1973 three archbishops (one of whom was Dom Helder Camara) and ten bishops in the North-east issued an outspoken document accusing the régime of arbitrary imprisonment and torture of its opponents. Quoting government figures of wages, unemployment and health conditions, the document described Brazil's so-called economic miracle as merely a means of making the rich richer and the poor poorer. Clearly this action did not enjoy the support of the Church hierarchy as a whole because it was not long before a Brazilian cardinal published a criticism of the document which he described as being couched in Marxist language.

The Church has a great role to play in the challenging conditions of a rapidly developing country like Brazil, and it can count on the services of many priests of high calibre to help carry out this work. In fulfilling its task, the Brazilian Church has the advantage of never having excited envy through the acquisition of wealth or property on any appreciable scale.

Friction with the State inevitably occurs, however, because the Church, in attempting to implement Vatican policy laid down in papal encyclicals, cannot avoid entering the political field when concerning itself with social problems in a developing country like Brazil.

HISTORICAL LANDMARKS

For a period of about thirty years after the discovery of Brazil in 1500 by the Portuguese navigator Pedro Alvares Cabral, this new colony was virtually ignored by Portugal since preliminary exploration appeared to show that the country contained no outstanding wealth. The Portuguese therefore rather lost interest in their new territorial acquisition and continued to devote their attention towards obtaining riches from the East. This attitude allowed speculators of other nationalities to develop a profitable trading business in wood with Brazil. They established themselves so well on the coast of Brazil that the Portuguese became alarmed and decided to adopt a firmer line towards their new colony. The Portuguese king, Dom João III, detailed a fleet of Portuguese ships to patrol the Brazilian coast; and in 1532 he divided Brazil into areas called *capitanías*, each under the command of leading Portuguese nobles and soldiers. The system did not work well and so in 1548 the king established a central government at what is now the city of Salvador, Bahia. It was not until 1763 that Rio de Janeiro became the sole capital of Brazil, and it remained as such for very nearly 200 years until 21 April 1960 when Brasilia was inaugurated as the new capital.

The first colonists settled along the coastal belt of Brazil, but soon the quest for minerals and other wealth attracted expeditions inland. In 1554 the Jesuits founded São Paulo do

Campo de Piratininga, the present city of São Paulo and industrial colossus of South America, and it was from here that *bandeiras* or expeditions set off for the hinterland in search of gold, diamonds, emeralds and Indian captives who could serve as slaves. Some of these expeditions penetrated immense distances into unknown territory and many of the explorers were away from home for several years. The members of one of the expeditions even walked from São Paulo to the Pacific and back; but they returned greatly depleted in numbers, due to sickness and attacks by hostile Indians who resisted such incursions into their traditional hunting grounds. These expeditions by the Paulistas gave rise to protests by the Spaniards who viewed such explorations as trespass on territory they regarded as theirs under the treaty of Tordesillas signed in 1494. By this treaty the Portuguese were permitted to explore and take possession of new lands only up to 370 leagues to the west of the Cape Verde Islands, while anything beyond that line was considered to be the property of the Spaniards. But the Paulistas paid little heed to imaginary lines.

There was a spate of frenzied prospecting in Brazil during the early eighteenth century after gold and diamonds were found in Minas Gerais, Goiás and Mato Grosso. These were the bonanza days and reports from Cuiabá (the present capital of the state of Mato Grosso) that a group of people near there had managed to find three tons of gold within the space of a month were enough to precipitate a tremendous rush to the area.

The hunting down of Indians was carried out relentlessly by the colonisers who needed forced labour, especially for the sugar plantations. But the captured Indians proved to be recalcitrant slaves and incapable of the exertions required of them. It was becoming more difficult, moreover, to make new captives since tribes had started to resist the white men once they realised that their visitors had come to stay. The Portuguese therefore imported African Negroes to Brazil and put them to work as slaves.

In the middle of the sixteenth century the French under

Villegagnon established themselves on an island in Rio de Janeiro bay and began colonisation with the idea of founding the city of Henriville on the mainland in honour of King Henri II of France. Attempts by the Portuguese to dislodge them were unsuccessful until 20 January 1567 when the opposing forces met in a hard-fought battle which took place near the site of the present Hotel Gloria in Rio. The French were defeated and, taking to their ships, they abandoned Brazil.

Occupation of North-east Brazil by the Dutch was more successful. By the end of the sixteenth century their ships were already raiding the coast and in 1595 they joined the English pirate James Lancaster to sack Pernambuco (now Recife) and occupy it for one month. The Dutch captured the city of Bahia (now Salvador) in 1624 but lost it in the following year. In 1630 they landed with a large force at Recife and over the next few years extended their dominion over a wide area of the North-east. Resistance to the Dutch occupation evaporated during the governorship of Prince Maurice of Nassau who ruled the colony from 1637 to 1644 with wisdom, tolerance and rare political and military acumen. But conditions changed after his departure, and as a result the seeds of resistance began to germinate. Insurrection broke out and culminated in the battle of Guararapes in 1649 when the local patriots defeated the Dutch forces, took many prisoners, and captured all the enemy artillery. The Dutch capitulated only in 1654, however, and agreed to lay down their arms and leave the country. It was not until 1661 that a peace treaty was signed in The Hague. There are several corrupt forms of names like Wanderley in Pernambuco today which serve as reminders of the past Dutch colonial imprint.

Resentment against Portuguese rule began to grow in Brazil among the colonists as they were called upon to pay higher and higher taxes, and the first separatist movement of note broke out in 1789 in the state of Minas Gerais. This was the *Inconfidencia Mineira* and its principal leader was Joaquim José da Silva Xavier whose nickname was Tiradentes (take out teeth) because he was a dentist. The movement was soon suppressed, the dentist was hanged and the other rebels were sent into exile in Africa. The rumblings of discontent continued in the colony, however, until 1808 when something totally unexpected occurred. This was the flight of the Portuguese royal family from Lisbon to Brazil in British ships to escape Napoleon's troops. The arrival of the royal visitors first in Salvador and then in Rio was welcomed with widespread joy and prolonged festivities, but the accommodation of such august personages and their vast retinue of courtiers posed serious problems to colonial towns providing amenities less sumptuous than those available in Lisbon.

In 1821 Dom João VI returned to Portugal after the French troops had abandoned Lisbon, and left his son Pedro behind in charge of the Brazilian colony. The Portuguese parliament wished Brazil to return to its former status of colony and called upon Dom Pedro to return to Portugal. This caused dissatisfaction in Brazil and finally decided Dom Pedro, acting on local support, to remain in Brazil and declare the country's independence. This he did on 7 September 1822 with the challenging cry of 'Independence or death' as he sat his horse on the banks of the river Ipiranga near the city of São Paulo. He is said to have then galloped the 260 miles to Rio, stopping only to change horses many times on the way. On 12 October 1822 he was proclaimed constitutional emperor of Brazil and on 1 December he was crowned in Rio de Janeiro. Brazil thus became an independent state.

Dom Pedro I had liberal ideas but his authoritarian character lost him popularity. As a result of a military revolt he abdicated in 1831 in favour of his son Pedro who was then only five years old. A regency council was set up and acted until 23 July 1840 when the young prince, now fifteen, was declared of age and became Dom Pedro II. In 1865 the country went to war against Paraguay and hostilities continued until 1870 when President Solano Lopez was defeated. Brazil now entered an era of great prosperity, but the starting of industries created difficulties for an economic structure based on slavery. A powerful emancipation movement resulted and on 13 May 1888 Princess Isabel, using a gold pen, signed an act abolishing slavery, a step which deprived the Empire of the support of the coffee- and sugar-planters. In the following year of 1889 a military movement proclaimed the republic and Marshal Deodoro da Fonseca was elected Brazil's first president. Dom Pedro II and the imperial family left Brazil to go into exile.

There were many political convulsions in the country before 1930 when Getulio Vargas, then Governor of the state of Rio Grande do Sul, came to power and ruled with dictatorial measures until 1934. There were parliamentary elections in that year and Congress maintained Vargas in power as constitutional president. In 1937 Vargas re-established his dictatorship by a *coup d'état* and his so-called New State lasted until after World War II when he was deposed. In the election which followed, General Eurico Gaspar Dutra was elected president. Vargas came back to the presidency in 1950; but a series of subsequent disturbances in the country finally led to the intervention of the armed forces and the suicide of Vargas on 24 August 1954.

Elections held on 3 October 1955 brought Dr Juscelino Kubitschek de Oliveira to the presidency and he assumed office on 31 January 1956, with Sr João Goulart as vice-president. During his term of office Dr Kubitschek stimulated the development of Brazil, but this was not achieved without considerable inflation. He will go down in history as the president who caused the new capital of Brasilia to be built. Some thought this action visionary while others maintain to this day that it was nothing but a foolish waste of effort and money.

In 1961 Sr Jánio da Silva Quadros became president of Brazil and once again Sr João Goulart was vice-president. After only a few months in office Sr Quadros resigned on 25 August 1961 and left Brazil three days later on board the British ship *Uruguay Star*. Constitutionally it was for Sr João Goulart to succeed him, but opposition to this step was raised in military circles. Sr João Goulart, who had been on a visit to China at the time when President Quadros had resigned, was sworn in as president on 7 September 1961 on the understanding that his powers would be limited by a parliamentary régime. However, a plebiscite called by President Goulart in 1963 re-established the presidential régime. The extreme left-wing policies of his government caused great political and social unrest coupled with galloping inflation which resulted in the 1964 revolution.

Beforehand, opposition to President Goulart's policies and actions had been building up, not only in the armed forces, but also among the majority of Brazilians who viewed the situation of continual strikes and unrest with increasing exasperation and alarm. Not long before the 1964 revolution there was a much publicised incident when the women of Belo Horizonte turned out en masse to protest against the political sympathies of Brizola, Goulart's brother-in-law and ultra-Leftist, when he was scheduled to give a lecture there. Wearing mantillas the women, some carrying candles and others telling their beads, invaded the lecture hall where they fell on their knees and prayed for the salvation of Brazil and of their families. Priests accompanied them. In the face of such determined though passive opposition, Brizola was forced to cancel his lecture. Unimportant though it may appear, this was a significant demonstration because it showed that the women of Brazil were mobilising against the régime and were a force to be reckoned with. Their open action of protest gave comfort and a sense of solidarity to millions of Brazilians who felt that, if things went on as they were going, the country would become communist. They realised now that they were not alone in their individual fears. The situation went from bad to worse and the armed forces decided to act.

The 1964 revolution caused half-a-dozen deaths and was over in twenty-four hours. It was set in motion when General Mourão and General Antonio Carlos Muricy started marching their troops down from Minas Gerais towards Rio de Janeiro, a movement against the central government which quickly brought open support from army commanders and most of the state governors. Miguel Arraes, the governor of Pernambuco, who was widely believed to have communist sympathies, refused to resign. He was accordingly deposed by the local armed forces commanders and sent from Recife into exile on the island of Fernando do Noronha off the north-east coast, together with others detained for political reasons. Some months later the authorities gave a splendid example of Brazilian benevolence by flying Miguel Arraes back to Recife for the inside of a day in order that he could be present at the wedding of one of his daughters.

Resistance to the revolution was negligible and the military were quickly in command of the country. It had become abundantly clear that the bulk of Brazilian opinion was in favour of the action taken by the armed forces and so President Goulart, soon finding that he enjoyed no popular support, fled to Uruguay. After it was all over, demonstrations and processions in the streets by huge crowds of Brazilians were held to celebrate the change that had taken place.

The 1964 revolution was a milestone in Brazilian history. The military, irked and disillusioned by the inadequacies and corruptness of the old political system, were determined to create conditions favouring orderly economic and social development even though the anti-inflationary and other measures they would have to take might prove unpopular. The military leaders acted in a spirit of patriotism and not for any motives of personal gain or political advancement.

Their choice for the new head of state was Marshal Humberto de Alencar Castelo Branco. He was installed as president on 15 April 1964 in Brasilia and within a short time was responsible for introducing measures to eliminate corruption and communist infiltration and to curb inflation. An austere man without relish for the personality cult, President Castelo Branco neither sought nor achieved personal popularity with the people, but he firmly took actions which he considered to be in the best interests of his country. When representations were made to him that a certain person should be retained in his post on the grounds that he was indispensable, President Castelo Branco is said to have replied: 'But the cemeteries are full of indispensable people.' His administration certainly devoted itself to establishing sound and stable bases for the development of Brazil. Marshal Castelo Branco was killed in an air accident soon after leaving the presidency on 15 March 1967.

He was succeeded by Marshal Artur Costa e Silva who had previously been Minister of War. Described as a bluff soldier from the state of Rio Grande do Sul, President Costa e Silva enjoyed greater personal popularity with the people and his policies were less stern. By now Brazil's rate of development was accelerating fast, especially in the field of transport and communications, in shipbuilding and in industry. Foreign investors began to show renewed confidence. In November 1968 Queen Elizabeth II paid a state visit to Brazil, a British Trade Fair was held in São Paulo early in the following year, and Anglo-Brazilian trade began to flourish again after a long period of stagnancy. Widespread shock was caused by the death of President Costa e Silva, while still in office, during the second half of 1969. After a short period during which the country was governed from 1 September 1969 by a junta of the three Ministers of the Armed Forces, General Garrastazu Medici was elected president by Congress and assumed office on 30 October 1969. His mandate ended on 15 March 1974.

A native of the state of Rio Grande do Sul like his immediate predecessor, President Medici led his country along the path of development with honesty and good sense coupled with firmness of purpose and a sympathetic way of dealing with people and situations. Never in the public eye before becoming president, he managed to gain a position where he was treated by most Brazilians with respect tinged by a kind of reverence. His period of office saw the introduction of such far-reaching plans as *Proterra*, a mammoth scheme to develop the impoverished North-east, and the first real implementation of agrarian reform. President Medici's personal popularity among his countrymen received a boost when Brazil's football team won the World Cup outright in 1970, almost as though he had been responsible for this success. At the time he was credited with having started the popular slogan: *Ninguem segura o Brasil* ('No one can hold back Brazil').

The Medici régime, being authoritarian, has naturally been the subject of controversy. Most of the criticisms levelled against it have come from outside Brazil, not from inside. Outside opponents have argued that the reason for this is that freedom of expression has been curtailed in Brazil under a military régime. It is true that newspapers are (at the time of writing) liable to censorship, but this does not mean that criticism of some of the actions and policies of the régime has not been made in the newspapers. Brazilians and foreigners living in the country are free to move about as they please, to live where they wish, and to work where they choose. Many ministers and other officials in high positions are civilians. The military have been ultimately in command of the situation in Brazil, but the accepted trappings of a military dictatorship have not been visible in the day-to-day life of the country or of its inhabitants.

True, conditions are difficult for communists and terrorists to plan and carry out activities against the government and they can expect short shrift. The position is that the military, who acted in 1964 to stop the increasing chaos in the country's economic and political life, believe that a strong régime is necessary in Brazil to introduce social reforms and to promote industrial and economic development. They have been committed to this course, without minding who gets hurt in the process. Brazil's phenomenal development over the last decade is testimony to the firmness of their belief and purpose.

The system has been described as 'directed democracy' and it is unlikely to be altered for some time to come. General Ernesto Geisel, who was head of President Castelo Branco's military household and later chairman of Petrobras (the State oil enterprise), was nominated in 1973 to take over from President Medici in March 1974. When announcing his approval of the selection of General Geisel as his successor, President Medici made it clear that the philosophy of the 'revolutionary order' would be continued under the next régime. While not expecting any major changes of basic policy to be made under the new régime, many observers believed, however, that General Geisel would allow Congress greater scope and permit wider political activity within the country during his term as president.

During 1971 Brazil was actively engaged in cementing relations both with its South American neighbours and with Portugal through official visits and negotiations. It also increased its territorial waters to 200 miles. The year 1972 was a special one for Brazil, being the 150th anniversary of its independence. That the remains of the emperor Pedro I should have been brought back to Brazil from Portugal to mark the occasion was a nice touch reflecting the respect which Brazil feels for its imperial family, both living and dead.

This attitude must appear paradoxical, but then the whole course of Brazilian political history is full of paradoxes. Nearly all Brazilian revolutions have been carried out, not with the object of destroying law and order as is usually the case with revolutions, but in the name of 'legalism', in order to restore law and order when the revolutionaries considered that the government of the time was outside the law. The prince regent declared Brazil's independence against the 'anarchical, factious, Machiavellian, horrible, pestiferous' courts of Lisbon on the grounds that Dom João VI was under compulsion and that the said assembly wished to destroy the united kingdom of Portugal. In 1889 Marshal Deodoro da Fonseca proclaimed the republic

---

A fishermen's colony at Ubatuba, state of São Paulo. Dugout canoes like these are still widely used by fishermen along the Brazilian coast. Sometimes they are driven by outboard motors

A view of the busy port of Santos, outlet for exports from São Paulo

'provisionally', not in revolt against the authority of the emperor but because the emperor of Brazil had no more authority. The following passage from the marshal's letter of 16 November 1889 to the sovereign respectfully asking him to leave the country sounds more like a communication from a dutiful subject than from one who had just taken over power:

. . . In view of this situation it rests with us to tell you, and we only do so in fulfilment of the most painful of duties, that the presence of the Imperial Family in the country in face of the new situation created by the irrevocable resolution of the 15th would be absurd, impossible, and liable to provoke sorrow which the public salvation imposes on us the need to avoid.

Obeying, therefore, the exigencies of the national vote, with all respect due to the dignity of the public functions you have finished exercising, we are forced to notify you that the provisional government expects from your patriotism the sacrifice of leaving national territory with your family in the shortest space of time possible.

To this end is established for you the maximum time limit of twenty-four hours which we count upon you will not attempt to exceed.

The transportation of you and yours to a port of Europe will be

---

Vaqueiros or cowboys hold an immense herd of *zebú* or Brahmin cattle. Cowboys usually wear leather trousers or aprons and ride on thick sheepskins over their saddles

Harvesting wheat in Southern Brazil. The girl wears comfortable clothes, a sensible hat, and slippers

D

for the account of the State, the provisional government providing you for that purpose with a ship and the necessary military crew, embarkation being carried out with the most absolute safety of your person and of all your family whose comfort and health will be watched over with the greatest diligence during the crossing, with you continuing to rely upon the endowment which the law assures you until the next Constituent Assembly pronounces upon that point.

All orders have been given for this determination to be carried out.

The country counts upon you knowing how to imitate in submission to its wishes the example of the first emperor on 7 April 1831.

The almost apologetic tone of this letter reflects a sense of guilt felt by Brazilians about the termination of their monarchy. Not many years went by before they allowed the descendants of the imperial family to return to Brazil where there now live two pretenders to a non-existent throne. There are those who still cherish the thought of Brazil's becoming a constitutional monarchy; but this idea, revolutionary though it may be, is probably completely outside the realms of possibility, even in the context of 'Brazilian solutions'.

2

The Regions

BRAZIL is divided into five geographic regions which are referred to as the North, North-east, South-east, South and Central West. The North, which is by far the biggest, is made up of the states of Amazonas, Pará, Acre, and the territories of Amapá, Roraima and Rondonia. The North-east comprises the states of Maranhão, Rio Grande do Norte, Piauí, Ceará, Pernambuco, Bahia, Alagoas, Paraiba, Sergipe and the territory of Fernando de Noronha (an island off the north-east coast). The South-east is made up of the states of Minas Gerais, São Paulo, Guanabara, Espírito Santo and Rio de Janeiro. The states of Paraná, Santa Catarina and Rio Grande do Sul make up the South, while the Central West, the second largest region, takes in the states of Mato Grosso, Goiás and the federal district.

Amazonia in the North covers three-fifths of the area of Brazil, two-fifths of the area of South America and a twentieth of the earth's land surface. As yet not a great deal is known about the quality of the soil there although it appears that much of it is infertile. At the beginning of the twentieth century the Amazonian economy began to boom as a result of exploitation of rubber and its high price on world markets. In 1820 natural rubber was sold at £67 (about US $167) a ton but in 1910 the price had risen to £655 (about US $1,637) a ton owing to world demand for this product. Production of rubber in Brazil, some hundreds of tons in 1820, rose to more than 40,000 tons in 1912 but by 1932 it had fallen to little more than 1,000 tons. Rubber production at the boom period of 1910 was worth £25 million (about US $62½ million) which represented 20 per cent of

Brazilian exports for that year. In 1932 Brazilian rubber exports were worth only £200,000 (about US $500,000) or 1 per cent of their value in 1910.

After the phase of rubber in the North came that of Brazil nuts which represented US $10 million (about £4 million) of Amazonian exports in 1964. Unlike the rubber tree, the Brazil nut tree did not have to face competitive production from commercial plantations of its own kind but it had to compete with the production elsewhere of other nuts such as cashew.

After the collapse of rubber prices between 1910 and 1912 the economy of Amazonia entered a period of acute recession which was not relieved until the 1930s, when the Japanese began cultivating jute there. In 1964 jute and its derivates accounted for 34 per cent of the total of exports from the state of Amazonas.

The planting of pepper was also started by the Japanese in Amazonia, principally in the state of Pará. In 1952 Brazil produced less than 400 tons of pepper, about 1 per cent of the world's total production, but by 1960 this figure had risen to 5,000 tons or 5 per cent of the world's production, making Brazil the world's fifth largest producer. The state of Pará was responsible for 80 per cent of Brazil's production, 80 per cent of which was exported to Argentina, Germany and the USA.

The North region has always been a producer of beef on the extensive system, but transportation of cattle coupled with a lack of packing-houses have been problems preventing any significant beef shipments out of the area. Cattle being carried on the lower decks of boats is still a regular feature of the Amazon river scene, but the building of new roads may alter this. Already large companies have opened up enormous grazing lands beside the Belém–Brasilia highway in areas which were previously considered to be too remote for exploitation; and now the transamazonian highway should have a similar effect.

The climate in the North region is uniformly hot and humid and heavy rains during much of the year cause serious soil erosion. Floods can have a disastrous effect upon the economy. Life is hard and the challenge great in the North, but those prepared to put up with the difficulties and discomforts in this developing area stand to make good profits. Certainly there is plenty of room for newcomers: according to the 1970 census there is a total population of only 3,650,750 in the whole of the vast North region, nearly two-thirds being in the state of Pará. Belém, capital of this state and principal port of the North, is developing fast and many new industries have been established there. Farther along the Amazon to the West is the free zone of Manaus, which was created in February 1967 with the object of industrialising the area. The free zone, which is on the left bank of the Negro and the Amazon rivers, covers an area of nearly 4,000 square miles, or about eight times the size of the state of Guanabara, and includes the city of Manaus and most of its municipality. There is a special system of franchise for the import into the free zone of goods, materials, raw materials and other products destined for internal consumption or industrialisation within the free zone or for the installation or operation of industries and services, warehousing of merchandise for re-export, or for commercialisation in other parts of Brazil. Passenger vehicles, tobacco, perfume, alcoholic drinks and guns and ammunition do not enjoy these special import privileges in the free zone of Manaus. A visitor to the city finds that he can buy all kinds of transistor radios, television sets and cameras at attractive prices; but there is a limit to what he is allowed to take out on departure from the airport where customs formalities are strict.

Whether or not the free zone of Manaus has yet achieved its object remains a matter of controversy. Authorities responsible for implementation of the scheme claim that twenty-three industrial projects for the area were approved in 1969, twenty in 1970 and more than another twenty in 1971. The incentives offered to any person or company setting up an industry in the free zone of Manaus before 1981 are certainly attractive and include up to 100 per cent income-tax exemption. Interest in the free zone scheme from other parts of Brazil, not overwhelming so far, may increase now that access to Manaus is being improved by the construction of new roads.

The North-east region has a population of 28,675,081 and its traditional capital is Recife. Although it is the area where the most extensive early colonisation took place, the North-east has developed very slowly from an industrial point of view. Most of the population has always been concentrated in the *zona da mata*, a warm and humid area lying along the coast from the state of Rio Grande do Norte to Bahia, where the rich soil yields sugar-cane and agricultural crops. For centuries sugar-cane has been the basis of the state of Pernambuco's economy, but now efforts are being made to modernise methods of production and to diversify agriculture. The average yield of cane in Pernambuco is about 50 tons per hectare, but yields of 118 tons have been achieved by planting special varieties in selected soils with overhead irrigation. Such methods will clearly allow the same amount of cane to be produced from less land and permit the planting of other crops on the surplus soil.

Next inland is the *agreste* ('rough' or 'aggressive') area where the climate and soil are drier than in the *zona da mata*. Farmers here grow a type of cactus called *palma* as feed for their cattle in normal dry seasons, but they may be forced to move herds to other areas if there is a prolonged drought. Water is scarce at the best of times and is usually brackish. Pastures here, emerald green after rain, are almost unrecognisably brown and parched during the dry season and resemble scorched earth if there is a drought.

Farther inland is the *sertão*, an arid region of stunted trees, sparse vegetation and minimal agricultural production. Adequate survival is all that one can expect in this area, since the land does not possess the necessary potential for anyone to become rich from it.

Great efforts are being made to develop the region, mainly through a government agency called SUDENE (Superintendency for the Development of the North-east) which has its headquarters in Recife. Companies from the South have been encouraged to invest there under the tax incentives scheme and many new industries and other enterprises have been started

as a result. Commercial growing of tropical fruit and its industrialisation are being developed. Fishing methods have been
modernised and refrigerated vessels based at Recife set out
regularly to catch *pargo* or red snapper in waters farther to the
North. Nevertheless, a considerable amount of fishing in coastal
waters is still carried out from picturesque *jangadas*. A typically
North-eastern craft, the *jangada* consists of a raft made from
shaped logs and fairly skims along under a triangular sail. Logs
used in its construction are cut from light *piuba* wood from the
Amazon forests. The biggest *jangada* carries a crew of four. It
is not known where the design came from originally; but at the
time of the discovery of Brazil such craft were reported by the
first colonisers to be in use by the Indians, who called the
triangular sail 'white tongue'. It is quite an alarming experience
to sail in a *jangada* for the first time since the craft is constantly
awash.

The way of life in the North-east is often rough, but North-
easterners are a tough breed of people. They never seem to lose
their tenacious affection for their home territory even though
circumstances, such as a prolonged drought, may force them
to migrate to other parts of Brazil in search of better working
conditions. Perhaps it is the sharpening influence of the constant
challenge of life in many parts of the North-east that accounts
for the fact that the region has produced great Brazilian writers
like Gilberto Freyre, Euclides da Cunha, Jorge Amado and
José de Alencar, as well as many notable painters and politicians.

The North-east also produced Virgulino Ferreira da Silva
who, better known as *Lampião* or Lantern, was Brazil's most
famous bandit. Born in 1898, he was raised as a cowboy and by
the time he was sixteen years old he had become quite famous
for breaking in horses and mules. He also played the accordion
and is said to have had talents as a composer. His real vocation
was killing people, however, and after committing his first
murder at the age of seventeen he never really looked back.
With a gang of sometimes as many as 150 cut-throats he roamed
the North-eastern states, always accompanied by his faithful

female companion nicknamed Maria Bonita or Pretty Mary, who had left her shoemaker husband, to share the bandit chief's uncomfortable and dangerous life in the wilds. Posses of police constantly chased *Lampião* but were unable to catch him: on the contrary, he usually caught them in ambush and shot them down. When not blowing his victims to bits with a 1908 model Mauser rifle or 9mm pistol he was fond of killing them with his 67cm long dagger. He was said to have killed ten police officers and more than 200 other ranks during his career. *Lampião* appeared to bear a charmed life and to have an extraordinary sixth sense which warned him of impending danger. Through treachery the police finally caught him on 28 July 1938 in his favourite hideaway, unarmed, and put a bullet through his head. Pretty Mary ran to him, but she too was killed, as were eight other bandits.

With 40,331,969 inhabitants, the South-east is the most populated of the five regions and the one that is by far the most developed from an industrial point of view. The state of Guanabara, which consists mainly of the city of Rio de Janeiro and its suburbs, is the second most important industrial centre in Brazil after São Paulo and is the main centre of finance, the press and tourism. The city's port handled more than 22 million tons of cargo in 1970 and its facilities are being improved and extended to provide export warehouses, more cold storage space, and a terminal station to handle containers. The estimated income per capita in the state of Guanabara is the highest in Brazil at the equivalent of nearly US $1,000 (about £400) and is about two and a half times higher than the national average.

Rio de Janeiro was first discovered on 1 January 1502 by the Portuguese navigator Gonçalo Coelho who, wrongly thinking that the bay was a river, named it 'River of January'. The 'marvellous city', as Rio is known in Brazil, enjoys one of the most beautiful natural settings in the world, grouping mountains, bay and beaches together in a lovely scenic arrangement. Views, so well captured by early painters like Debret and Rugendas, are dramatic and never tiring to the eye of the observer. The distinctive Sugar Loaf mountain, 1,230ft at its highest point, crouches protectively at the entrance to the bay while 2,300ft above the city the 130ft high figure of Christ on the Corcovado or Hunchback mountain spreads its arms in an eternal benediction. The beaches of Copacabana, Arpoador and Ipanema form the playground of Rio and the forest of Tijuca is a pleasant retreat of coolness in the hot summer weather.

The sheer face of the Sugar Loaf rock must have presented a stirring challenge to climbers, but it was not until 1817 that the peak was first scaled. The first person to have reached the top is supposed to have been a thirty-nine-year-old English-woman named Henrietta Carsteirs. Her patriotic action of planting a British flag at the summit is reported to have angered a soldier or sergeant by the name of José-Maria Gonçalves, who considered her action to be an insult to Portugal. The next day, after a hard climb lasting six hours, he was able to remove the British flag and replace it with that of Portugal. For some inexplicable reason he was then dismissed from the army.

A similar incident occurred in 1838 when two British officers climbed the rock and left a British flag at the summit. Once again it was removed. In the same year a rockclimber named America Vespuci got to the top, thus making it two all for the ladies, not counting the Portuguese soldier. In 1851 a group of ten people, English and Americans, climbed the Sugar Loaf and spent the night on the summit. The group included two women and a ten-year-old boy and the boy is said to have been the first to reach the top.

Another twenty-six years went by before other foreigners climbed the Sugar Loaf and this time the party consisted of three Englishmen. Under watching Brazilian eyes they reached the top and won all hearts by planting the Brazilian flag there. This action must surely have eradicated any rankling ill-feeling about the patriotism of Miss Carsteirs in 1817. Some years later a team of students from a military school climbed the Sugar Loaf and unfurled a huge Brazilian flag in salute to Emperor Pedro II as he passed by in a steamer on return from Europe.

No one seems to be certain about the origin of the name Sugar Loaf. A popular version is that the conical rock looked like the sugar bricks made by cane-planters in the North-east of Brazil. The French found *pot à beurre* a suitable description, while English sailors in the eighteenth century were said to have detected a marked likeness between the outline of the Sugar Loaf and the profile of Admiral Lord Hood. Some Frenchmen, perhaps not to be outdone, thought it was similar to the profile of Louis XVI. Writers have claimed that the name stems from *pan-ad-acu-qua*, an Indian word said to mean 'the pointed hill on its own'. *Pão de açucar* is the Brazilian word for it.

The aerial cableway from the ground to the rump of the Sugar Loaf was inaugurated in October 1912 and in January of the following year the link to the peak was completed. New cables and cable-cars went into operation in 1972 to provide a better service. No visit to Rio can be complete without the experience of 'going up the Sugar Loaf' in order to appreciate the marvellous vista of the city and bay laid out below.

Traffic conditions in Rio became increasingly difficult during 1972 and 1973 due to widespread excavation work for the construction of the city's métro system and Cariocas will heave a sigh of relief when the work is finished. Many of them feel that a métro is unnecessary and that the creation of a monorail train system would have caused less chaos and provided the answer to commuters' transport problems.

Across the bay of Guanabara from the city of Rio de Janeiro is Niteroi, capital of the state of Rio. Large areas of this state are devoted to traditional agricultural production based on sugar-cane, rice, coffee and beef raising, while in some areas there is market-gardening, fruit-growing and milk-production. One of the most impressive examples of this state's industry is Volta Redonda, the largest steelworks in Latin America.

In the state of Minas Gerais, which is larger than France, there is considerable industrial development around the capital of Belo Horizonte which has grown rapidly to become the third city of Brazil. This state is well known for its iron ore and other mining industries as well as for extensive livestock and agricultural production. The charming town of Ouro Preto (Black Gold), situated about sixty miles from Belo Horizonte, has such a wealth of colonial architecture and painting that it was decreed a national monument in 1933. In the eighteenth century it was the home of Aleijadinho (Little Cripple), Brazil's most famous sculptor, and magnificent examples of his work can be seen in Ouro Preto and in the town of Congonhas do Campo. The state of Minas Gerais is also known for its spas of which Caxambú, São Lourenço, Poços de Caldas and Araxá are among the most frequented.

The economy of the state of Espírito Santo is based mainly on traditional livestock-breeding and agricultural activities. The port of Vitória, the capital of the state, is an important point for the import of coal and the export of iron ore, timber and coffee. It is also a fishing base.

The state of São Paulo is the most highly developed state of Brazil in regard to education, industry, agriculture, market-gardening and fruit-growing, roads, and electricity. Foreign immigrants established themselves here on a massive scale and their influence on the economy and the way of life has been profound in many areas.

The population of the city of São Paulo grew from 2,269,703 in 1960 to 5,978,977 in 1970, a figure representing 6·34 per cent of the total population of Brazil. The fastest growing city in the world, São Paulo looks like a forest of skyscrapers to the air traveller arriving at the city's airport of Congonhas. There is a distinct atmosphere of hustle and bustle in São Paulo and one can sense that the place is a beehive of activity; but things can be different at the rush hour when monster traffic jams reduce everything to a standstill and frustrated motorists blow angry symphonies on their horns. Pollution is also becoming a problem. Expansion has been too swift and it is small wonder that exasperated Paulistas have invented the slogan: 'São Paulo *has* to stop.'

The state of São Paulo accounts for about half of Brazil's industrial, and more than 40 per cent of its agricultural, output. It also produces large percentages of Brazil's textiles, electrical materials, chemicals and pharmaceuticals, cotton, sugar, rice, coffee, fruit exports, machinery and tools, and is responsible for more than 80 per cent of the country's production of motor vehicles. The port of Santos, about forty miles away, is the main point of export for goods from São Paulo. It can be reached by rail or by the spectacular Anchieta highway which winds down from a plateau at 2,000ft altitude to the great plain below.

Although it is the smallest in area of the five regions of Brazil, the South is larger than the whole Iberian peninsula. Its population, according to the September 1970 census figures, was 16,683,551 or 17·65 per cent of Brazil's total population. The region received small attention during early colonial days because there appeared to be little gold there and the soil was unsuitable for the production of sugar. The first immigrants to settle in coastal areas were families from the Azores who arrived in the eighteenth century. They were followed after Brazil's independence by settlers from Europe, mainly Germans, Italians and Slavs, who established themselves in small agricultural properties which they worked on their own (the use of slaves was forbidden there) and, more recently, people of other nationalities, including the British and the Dutch, founded communities because they were attracted by favourable farming conditions in the South region and by its pleasant subtropical climate. Industries have been started in the region but on the whole the basic economy remains agrarian. Products include meat, rice, wool, wine, wood, milk, wheat, mate tea, maize, potatoes and coffee.

Planned development is being carried out in the state of Paraná on an impressive scale and it will not be long before this state becomes one of the most important factors in Brazil's economy. The great social and economic progress being made there typifies the capacity of the South and the vitality of its inhabitants.

The vast Central West region covers an area of nearly 750,000 square miles and is populated by little more than 5 million people, including over 500,000 in Brasilia and the federal district. The states of Mato Grosso and Goiás have always been the Far West of Brazil, a land of Indians, gold-rushes, great open cattle-ranges, canyons, hunters, explorers, frontier towns and the ·44 Winchester carbine. This is still a largely true picture of the area today and it is unlikely to change for many years to come even though air and road communications are being improved. The region, where there are already more than 20 million head of cattle, can become one of the most important meat-producing centres in the world. There are already great ranches like the Fazenda Bodoquena where 85,000 head of cattle are run and where grass-seed is sown from small aircraft to form new pastures. Land is measured in leagues and a field of 200 acres is nothing but a small paddock. Tough Mato Grosso cowboys in the *pantanal*, or marshlands, wear leather aprons as protection against the searing effect of rawhide lariats running out on a galloping steer and hip-length leather boots reminiscent of those used by King Charles I and his cavaliers, or the American cowboys of the Plains. Old scores are still settled by the knife or by the gun. A Wild West atmosphere still prevails in remoter parts of the Central West region, but living and pay conditions have improved for many of the inhabitants. Although the region is essentially agricultural, cities like Cuiabá, Campo Grande, Goiánia and Anápolis are developing and beginning to make their presence felt from the point of view of the country's economy.

For more than half a century the state of Mato Grosso has held an especial fascination for foreigners as a place containing all the ingredients of adventure such as savage Indians, unexplored jungles, wild animals, tough hunters and lost cities. Much of the romantic atmosphere about it was created by three foreigners whose exploits captured the imagination of people outside Brazil.

During 1913–14 Colonel Theodore Roosevelt, accompanied by General Rondon who was then head of the Brazilian Indian Protection Service, carried out his South American expedition for the American Museum of Natural History through the wilds of Mato Grosso, a difficult and often dangerous journey on foot and by canoe which brought them into contact with several

tribes of Indians. Exploration by the expedition of the river
Duvida (Doubt) resulted in the river's being renamed Roosevelt. Colonel Roosevelt afterwards published a book called
Through the Brazilian Wilderness, describing his adventures. It was
a courageous effort for someone unfamiliar with local conditions
to undertake a journey of this nature, especially in those days.

Another foreigner, this time a Russian, whose activities in
Mato Grosso became famous, was Sasha Siemel. Better known
as Tiger Man, he was the first and probably still the only
foreigner to have killed jaguars with a spear, on foot and alone.
He was taught the skill by a Guató Indian named Joaquim and
he became a master of this dangerous profession requiring
iron courage and personal fortitude of a singular kind. Tiger
Man's experiences during his thirty years in the Brazilian jungle
remain unique.

It was probably an Englishman, Colonel Percy Harrison
Fawcett, however, who drew most attention to Mato Grosso and
its hidden mysteries through his several expeditions in search of
a lost city which he was convinced existed. He believed himself
to be probably the only person possessing knowledge of its
location somewhere in the Brazilian hinterland.

Colonel Fawcett was lost on his last expedition and no definite
clue to his disappearance has ever been found. In April 1925
he set off from Cuiabá, the capital of the state of Mato Grosso,
with his son Jack and another young Englishman named Raleigh
Rimmell. After about three weeks the expeditionaries, who had
pack-animals with them, arrived at the Bacairy Indian post
which in those days was the last outpost of civilisation on the
edge of unexplored territory. After resting for a few days, Colonel
Fawcett and his two companions pressed on into the wilds and
never returned. They are believed to have reached a village of
the Kalapalo Indians on the river Kuluene and to have gone on
from there. The Indians saw smoke from their fires for several
days and then these signs of the expedition's progress suddenly
ceased, thus implying that Colonel Fawcett and his companions
had been massacred. That is one story. Another version is that
Colonel Fawcett and his party were killed by the Kalapalo

Indians because of an incident which occurred in their village. According to this story, an Indian picked up the colonel's rifle in the spirit of curiosity that Indians have about white men's possessions but Fawcett, who was in a bad temper, snatched it back angrily. This action was considered to be an insult to a member of the tribe and so next day, when Fawcett and his companions were travelling in the Kalapalo canoes, they were clubbed to death.

For years the mysterious disappearance of the members of the expedition has been a subject for undiminished speculation and there are even those who believe that the colonel is still alive somewhere in Mato Grosso as a captive of hostile Indians, though he would now be well over 100 years old. A person who clings to this theory is the widow of one of Fawcett's ex-guides who has in her possession what is almost certainly the colonel's gold signet ring. It seems highly improbable that Colonel Fawcett will ever return, but perhaps one day his dreams and beliefs will be vindicated by the discovery of his lost city.

THE NEW CAPITAL OF BRASILIA

Brasilia, the fabulous new capital of Brazil, is the twentieth-century execution of an eighteenth-century idea. Many people are surprised to discover that the concept of siting the capital on the Central Plateau dates back to 1750, when the cartographer Francisco Tossi Colombina indicated the present location of the federal district as the most suitable place for the seat of government of the colony belonging to Portugal. There were others who wished to move the capital away from the coast. Those taking part in the abortive *Inconfidencia Mineira* revolution in 1789 wanted to establish it at São João del Rei in the state of Minas Gerais. One who crusaded in 1808 for the transference of the capital to the geographical centre of the country was Hipólito José da Costa Furtado de Mendonça. He had founded the newspaper called *Correio Braziliense* and was producing it in exile in London at that time. It is now the daily newspaper of Brasilia and retains the English *z* in *Braziliense* for old times' sake. A suggestion in favour of moving the capital was also made by William Pitt when he was British Ambassador to Portugal.

A serious and farsighted plan for the moving of the capital to the interior of the country was put forward in 1823 to the Constituent and Legislative General Assembly of the Empire by José Bonifácio de Andrade e Silva, who had already suggested two years previously that the new city to serve as the seat for the court or the regency should be built in a healthy and fertile place inland on about latitude 15°. His arguments were sound. He pointed out that siting the government in the centre of the country would make it safe from attack; that communications with the rest of the country would be better; that the construction of roads to the new capital would stimulate internal trade; and that unemployed sectors of the population on the coast would be attracted to, and absorbed by, the new capital. He even suggested that the new city should be called Brasilia. His plan, like others put up on similar lines by later visionaries, was pigeon-holed.

But the seeds of the idea had at least taken root and the first delicate tendrils of the plant were given strength by later governments of Brazil. In November 1892 the so-called Cruls Mission completed its allotted task of marking out the boundaries of the future federal district; but it was not until 7 September 1922 that the foundation stone of the new capital was laid in Brasilia at the place then known as Sitio Castanho. Nothing very positive happened until 1955 when the government of the state of Goiás disappropriated the area of the future federal district, declaring the land to be of public usefulness and advantageous to the interests of society. It was President Juscelino Kubitschek who applied the final touches. On 18 April 1956 in the city of Anápolis he signed a message to Congress asking for permission to move the federal capital and suggesting Brasilia as its name. This proposal was approved unanimously by the Chamber of Deputies and the Senate and was sanctioned by Law No 2,874 of 19 September 1956.

In early November 1956 the first pioneers arrived in the

hinterland to build the city of Brasilia. It is said that roads to the site were so rudimentary in those days that bricks had to be dropped in by parachute. The construction workers, many of whom came from the North-east of Brazil, were given the name of Candangos, a word used by the Bantu in Angola to describe the Portuguese. No one seems to know how and why the name Candango was applied to the Brasilia pioneers but it seems probable that the term was imported from Bahia. The name was like a decoration, signifying courage and pioneering spirit. Living in encampments without physical comforts, the Candangos certainly had to rough it, but everyone worked feverishly on the construction of the new capital as if inspired by the challenge and the ideal. News of this trail-blazing on the Central Plateau attracted an avalanche of new arrivals from all over Brazil. Some wanted to work, others to trade and there were those who catered for the off-duty pleasures of the cooped-up Candangos. Almost overnight a city blossomed to house them and provide for their needs. Situated near the present Brasília–Belo Horizonte road, it was called the Nucleo Bandeir-ante or, more familiarly, the Free City. It was an oasis for the workers and a breeding-ground for private enterprise. The Free City was due to be eliminated after an allotted span of existence, but all efforts to dislodge it have failed. Its roots and inhabitants are so tenacious that it may well have to become a satellite town of Brasilia eventually.

On 3 May 1957 President Kubitschek made his first official visit to the Sitio Castanho, an occasion when the Cardinal Archbishop of São Paulo, Dom Carlos Carmelo de Vasconcelos Mota, celebrated the first Mass in Brasilia. On 1 October 1957 the Law establishing 21 April 1960 as the official inauguration date of the new capital was sanctioned.

The federal district covers a large area of more than 2,000 square miles. The population of the city of Brasilia and its seven satellite towns, all within about thirteen to twenty-six miles from it, is a little more than 500,000.

Twenty-six projects for the layout of the future city of Brasilia were submitted in an open competition and it was that of Lúcio

E

Costa, a brilliant Brazilian urban planner, which won the day. His 'Pilot Plan' for the design of Brasilia has the ground outline of an aeroplane. The residential and business areas are located along the 'wings' and along the 'fuselage' are the government offices, military quarters, and the cultural, banking, hotel and recreational centres. Sited at the 'cockpit' is the Place of the Three Powers represented by the Executive and Legislative Bodies and the Supreme Court. The railway terminal, the market centre and the industrial area are alongside the 'tail'. The city's residential area consists of a large number of 'neighbourhood units', each comprising four 'superquadra' blocks of apartments. The plan was for each unit to cater for all the main needs of its dwellers in the shape of hospitals, schools, markets, churches and shopping centres. Next to the city is the Paranoá artificial lake which is about fifty miles long and three miles across at its widest point.

There is a certain sameness about the residential blocks and the flat-roofed shops, but much of Brasilia's architecture is of exceptionally bold design. The Palácio dos Arcos, where the Ministry of External Relations is installed, must be one of the most beautiful modern buildings in the world; and the president's official residence, called the Palácio da Alvorada, is also lovely. Both the cathedral and the theatre are of most unusual and striking design. The somewhat ramshackle terminal building at the airport has been replaced by a splendid new one which provides all facilities and comforts for air travellers. An unusual feature of the airport restaurant is the method of charging for food from the cold buffet. When a customer has made his selection his plate is put on a weighing-machine and the food is charged for by weight.

Car owners in Brasilia usually drive incredibly long distances every month just going about their business in and around the city. There are no traffic-lights or cross-roads to cause holdups. The advanced road pattern of the city is said to have created problems for followers of Macumba or voodoo since an important part of their ritual is the placing of lighted candles at a cross-roads before a session is held.

The visitor arriving in Brasilia for the first time finds that everything seems a little unreal in this ultra-modern city situated on an empty plateau 800 miles from Rio de Janeiro. Cynics have called it 'the other side of the moon' or 'the architectural frame awaiting a city'. The city is there all right but it is too young as yet to have acquired much soul or character or many distinctive smells of its own. Perhaps its very modernity and prearranged layout may prevent it from ever doing so.

For many years the half-finished city of Brasilia was like a waif because a large number of Brazilians resented the policy of moving the capital and the cost of building the new city. Many officials, accustomed to the flesh-pots and amenities of Rio, were reluctant to move to Brasilia and they often had valid reasons for their attitude. Some of them, for example, had apartments in Rio and sent their children to local schools. Transfer to Brasilia meant a complete change in their system of living. The challenge was finally accepted, however, not always with joy but at least with acquiescence. A joke was soon made about it. 'Brasilia is like Paradise,' Brazilians said, 'we all want to go there eventually but not just yet.'

There was a certain amount of one-upmanship between embassies to show willingness to move to Brasilia before the deadline set by the authorities for September 1972. Brazilian newspapers reported that the Dutch ambassador, after being bitten by a poisonous *jararaca* snake at a reception in Brasilia (before the deadline) announced on his way to hospital: 'This will at least prove that I am in Brasilia.' Several ambassadors still in Rio were said to have seized upon this unfortunate incident as a means of showing that transfer to the new capital should be delayed on the grounds that diplomatic life there was not yet without danger. But such arguments were of no avail.

The government took vigorous measures to move ministries and other official departments to Brasilia and foreign embassies followed suit. Many people have found, to their surprise, that they enjoy living in Brasilia. The city, beautiful though immature, evokes a kind of tolerant affection from many of its inhabitants, particularly from those old hands who have lived in Brasilia since the birth of the city. When an old hand is asked whether he was a *pioneiro* (pioneer) he is liable to confound his audience by describing himself as a *piotário*. This word, which does not exist in any dictionary, is a cross between *pioneiro* and *otário*, which means 'idiot' or 'nincompoop'. The old hand then goes on to explain that *piotário* describes those like himself who went to Brasilia as pioneers and were sufficiently idiotic to remain there. This denigratory comment usually means that the speaker really enjoys living in Brasilia.

An eminent Brazilian who has spent many years in Brasilia has been quoted as having said that life there is a cycle of six Ds. On arrival, he said, one was overcome by the first D of Dazzlement. This phase soon gave way to Disappointment which was quickly followed by Disillusion. Despair then set in. Divorce came next. When the final stage of Dementia was reached, he said, it meant that the individual was really rather beginning to enjoy life in Brasilia.

3

How the Country Is Run

BRAZILIAN political, economic and social institutions underwent considerable change after the 1964 revolution when the Castelo Branco government came to power and brought in measures to adapt these institutions to the country's development requirements. Changes were accomplished first by special acts, then by special laws and finally by a new constitution which came into effect on 15 March 1967, the date when Marshal Costa e Silva became president. The new constitution remodelled Brazil's institutional structure and strengthened the powers of the president while at the same time limiting those of Congress in some matters. The new constitution provided for indirect election of the president by an electoral college composed of Congress and representatives of the State Legislative Assemblies. It gave power to the president, in cases of emergency or in the public interest, to sign decree laws on matters of national security or public interest, subject to later approval by Congress. The president has authority to intervene in the affairs of any of the twenty-two states without consulting Congress and the right to declare a state of siege and rule by decree. Both the president and the vice-president are elected for a term of five years by an electoral college.

The new constitution also introduced reforms in the tax laws, housing, land and farming, banking, the financial market, labour, social security and the civil service. It contains modern democratic principles in regard to individual rights and guarantees. Under it both Brazilians and foreign nationals resident in Brazil are assured inviolability of life, freedom, security and the right of ownership within the terms specified. All citizens are declared equal before the law without distinction of sex, race, occupation, religion or political convictions. The constitution guarantees the free expression of thought and of political or philosophical convictions but forbids war propaganda, subversion of order, and class and racial prejudice. It states that the representational democratic régime is based on the plurality of parties and on the preservation of the fundamental rights of Man.

There is a federal form of government and legislative power is exercised by a Chamber of Deputies in collaboration with a Federal Senate. The Chamber of Deputies has representatives elected on the proportional system and the Federal Senate is made up of three representatives from each state elected by direct suffrage for a term of eight years. Congress legislates on all matters of federal competence, especially on taxes, the budget, credit operations, public debt, currency issues, and national and regional plans and programmes. The constitution provides that whenever the president so requests it, Bills must be debated by the Chamber of Deputies within forty-five days of their presentation, the same applying to the Senate. If no motions have been introduced within this period, then Bills will be automatically considered approved. In cases of extreme urgency and at the president's decision, Bills must be approved within forty days at a joint meeting of Congress. On some occasions in past years Congress held up Bills by simply not debating them and hence it is clear why these rules were introduced.

The Congress building in Brasilia is something out of the ordinary from an architectural point of view, but it in no way looks out of place in the ultra-modern capital of Brazil where the planners and designers were given a free rein to construct a new city in what was previously the middle of nowhere. Occupying a prominent position on the so-called Esplanade of Ministries, the tall administration building of Congress stands flanked on either side by two cup-like structures. One of these buildings, which houses the Senate, is downturned while that of the Chamber of Deputies resembles a teacup. Brazilian wits maintain that this design is symbolic. The 'bowl' housing the Chamber of Deputies is open at the top, they say, in order that all the aromas of the excellent ideas and proposals which are released should flow freely upwards, while the downturned 'bowl' next door represents the clamping-down on all these aromas once they reach the Senate.

POLITICAL PARTIES

A great number of political parties have existed in Brazil at one time or another, but many of them failed to achieve much significance or expression on a national level. Three important and influential parties were the Brazilian Labour Party (PTB) and the Social Democratic Party (PSD), both of which were created by President Getulio Vargas, and also the more right-wing National Democratic Union (UDN). At one time there was a neo-Nazi party in Brazil whose members were called *Integralistas*.

The business of politics in Brazil prior to the 1964 revolution was a constant issue and one which occupied the time and efforts of innumerable people who stood to gain by being on the winning side. Many methods were used during the electioneering campaign. One of the most astute was that allegedly employed by a candidate who clearly disposed of considerable funds. He would arrive at a town and, so it is said, strike bets with all and sundry that he would *not* be elected. The candidate made a point of having all the bets registered with a notary public in order to satisfy any doubts which his challengers may have had about the firmness of his intentions to pay if elected. When election day came it was no surprise when this candidate was voted in on an overwhelming majority by those who subsequently collected the money from their bets. But the new member could not really be officially accused of bribery among the electorate. He was just clever enough to have had the *jeito* and others perhaps kicked themselves for not having thought of the idea first.

After the 1964 revolution in Brazil President Castelo Branco took the radical step of abolishing all political parties. This action, which was perhaps horrifying to some outside observers at the time, did not cause much shock to Brazilians since many of them felt that it was high time the old political party system was modified even by such methods of major surgery. After wiping the slate clean, the government laid down rules for the creation of new political parties. Two were then formed on a national basis, one being the pro-government *Aliança Renovadora Nacional*, usually referred to as ARENA, and the other the opposition party called *Movimento Democrático Brasileiro* (MDB). Under the constitution the organisation, operation and extinction of political parties are regulated by federal law. Political parties must be permanently active and their aims must be approved by the Supreme Electoral Court. They must in no way be associated with foreign governments, organisations or political parties; and they are subject to auditing. They are also subject constitutionally to the prohibition of party coalition.

Some tentative moves were made in 1971 by certain politicians with the idea of forming a third party, but they did not meet with much enthusiasm on a national scale. Since 1964 most of the old fire has gone out of Brazilian party politics because there is no longer the interest in them which existed before the revolution. This is not simply because an authoritarian régime came to power in 1964 and modified the political structure. There has also been a change of mood among Brazilians as a result of the rapid economic growth and development of their country in recent years. Achievements by the technocrats now capture their imagination more than do the speeches of politicians, however well the latter may represent their constituents and contribute by work in their own field towards Brazil's progress. The old-time world of party political infighting in Brazil must be beyond the comprehension of the young generation who have grown up in the age of technocrats where men land on the moon.

During President Goulart's régime his extreme Leftist policies permitted Brazilian communists to secure positions of influence in the government and trade unions and also to infiltrate the armed forces. When the Brazilian military carried out the 1964 revolution many communists were arrested and others fled the country, with the result that the Brazilian Communist Party (PCB) was thrown into disarray. The Brazilian Communist Party, which is proscribed, follows the Moscow line. There are also other parties formed by splinter groups dedicated to violent methods and these include the Communist Party of Brazil (PCdoB), which follows the Chinese line, and the Revolutionary Brazilian Communist Party (PCBR). There are also several terrorist organisations which have achieved notoriety through kidnappings, assassinations and armed robberies, but they do not enjoy the sympathy or support of the Brazilian people. By kidnapping in turn the United States ambassador, the West German ambassador, and the Swiss ambassador, the Brazilian terrorists were able to secure the release of many political prisoners. However, their cause suffered severe setbacks when their three principal leaders died as a result of police actions in 1970 and 1971.

Brazilian terrorists have been responsible for several cold-blooded murders, including that of the American Captain Chandler, who was machine-gunned in his car outside his home in São Paulo before the eyes of his children. Such actions, coupled with the kidnapping and imprisonment on political grounds of foreign ambassadors, created no sympathy for the terrorists' cause among the Brazilian people. On the contrary, the general reaction was one of shock and revulsion. Counter-action by the authorities has been swift, ruthless and determined. Few can hold any illusions that captured terrorists are handled with kid gloves by the authorities.

The Brazilian régime has been accused of torturing political prisoners. There can be little doubt in the minds of most people, Brazilians included, that there is a basis for such allegations; but it is stretching the imagination too far to believe that any such incidents have been part of a deliberate government policy. The most widely held opinion is that torture, if it has taken place, has been carried out by individual members of the police or security forces for sadistic reasons or for the quick extraction of information. This explanation is of course no justification for torture. Several cases of excesses committed by the police have been reported by Brazilian newspapers, and it is significant that the commander of the military police in São Paulo distributed an official note in March 1973 stating that he was taking action to stop cases of abuse by the police and to punish those concerned. He added that 1,031 members of the São Paulo military police had been dismissed from the force in 1972.

LOCAL GOVERNMENT

In Brazilian states executive power is exercised by governors and their secretaries of state, while legislative power is exercised by legislative assemblies who legislate on all matters affecting provincial administration, including the levying of taxes for state needs and expenditure. They also legislate on civil and criminal affairs affecting their own territory.

Municipal governments are autonomous in matters of local interest and are constituted by a mayor (*prefeito*) and a council of aldermen (*vereadores*). Administrative activities including those of a financial nature are carried out under the general provisions laid down in the municipal basic law.

THE CURRENCY

Brazil's currency based on the decimal system is the cruzeiro unit, divided into 100 centavos, which superseded the milreis. Notes are issued for 1, 5, 10, 50, 100 and 500 cruzeiros and coins for 1, 2, 5, 10, 20 and 50 centavos and 1 cruzeiro. Previous to 1964 the present 1 cruzeiro was 1,000 cruzeiros, but the currency's steady depreciation caused the Castelo Branco government to lop off the noughts and to introduce the new cruzeiro in much the same way that the new franc was introduced in

France. For a considerable time afterwards the currency of Brazil had to be referred to in writing (on cheques, for instance) as ncr or new cruzeiros, but as from 15 May 1970 the currency previously designated new cruzeiro became the cruzeiro and it is now written in its abbreviated form as cr instead of ncr. Nevertheless, there are still many old cruzeiro notes in circulation, some of them overprinted with their current value, although they are gradually being withdrawn.

Newcomers to Brazil may find it confusing when old-time residents talk about *contos* in terms of money. The old 1,000 cruzeiros (now 1 cruzeiro) was usually referred to as a *conto* until fairly recent times and those brought up with this popular denomination find it difficult to discard the term in favour of the modern 1 cruzeiro. This clinging to past terminology is probably motivated by a feeling of nostalgia or *saudade* for the good old monetary conversion days in Brazil (and not so long ago at that) when the *conto* was worth over £20 (about US $50). Alas, the *conto* or modern 1 cruzeiro will now buy only two small cups of coffee and 6 cruzeiros can no longer buy 40p (about US $1). Many people still talk in terms of old rather than new millions in relation to the cruzeiro. If they say something is worth a million old then this means 1,000 cruzeiros by modern standards or just under £70 (about US $175). No doubt with time these terms will, like old soldiers, simply fade away.

Over the past twenty years the Brazilian currency has depreciated greatly in value and the cruzeiro has suffered periodic devaluations by such dramatic amounts as 20 per cent at a time. Recent Brazilian governments adopted a different policy, however, which led to the cruzeiro's being devalued fairly regularly by small amounts. This policy of 'a little at a time and fairly often' has allowed the economy to absorb the shock effects more easily than was possible in the days of dizzying devaluation coupled with galloping inflation.

Brazilian bank-notes are printed nowadays by the *Casa da Moeda*, which is the Brazilian Mint. Many of the notes portray Tiradentes at the gallows, some show Dom Pedro I and II (a nice touch in a republic), but most present the head and shoulders of Santos Dumont wearing a high collar and a floppy hat. On the back of this note is a picture of an early flying machine, presumably that flown by this great Brazilian pioneer of aviation whose exploits are probably not as well known outside Brazil as they deserve to be.

TAXATION

It is only in the last ten years that tax declaration and collection in accordance with the rules and regulations has become an accepted practice in Brazil. Previously it was a rather haphazard affair and most people found fairly easy ways and means of avoiding payment of taxes or at least a sizeable percentage of them. Strict measures imposed by governments which have been in power since the revolution of 1964 caused the situation to change radically in this respect and the number of people making annual tax declarations has risen meteorically. It is not only the penalties which have been introduced for lack of compliance with the tax regulations or the improved system of collection that changed the Brazilians' attitude to tax payments, but also a newborn confidence that administrations would now ensure that tax money was applied in a proper manner.

Only individuals earning more than 1,325 cruzeiros net per month after deduction of allowances were liable for income tax deducted at source during 1972. Income tax due on monthly salaries above this amount was calculated on a sliding scale with allowances for dependants, pension and other specified payments being deductable from the gross sum to arrive at the taxable amount. Monthly tax due on a monthly income of 2,000 cruzeiros after deductions was 49·59 cruzeiros, while that on 3,697 was 240·35. Tax on incomes higher than this last figure was calculated on the basis of 15 per cent of the total net income after deduction of allowances, less the sum of 314·20 cruzeiros. Thus the monthly tax payable on a net monthly income of 5,248 cruzeiros was 473. An interesting angle on income tax collection is that those who pay without delay get a discount while the laggards have fines imposed upon them.

The change of attitude towards income tax has been such, so it is said, that social butterflies who were prepared in slap-happy tax days to pay social columnists to publish news of their champagne parties, world-wide travels or acquisition of expensive motor-cars, were soon clamouring to pay in order that such details should *not* be printed. Otherwise the tax-man might come round and ask embarrassing questions.

In the late 1950s a novel tax-measure was introduced called 'fiscal incentives'. This allows individuals and companies to apply a certain percentage of their income tax to enterprises considered by the government to be of national interest. Thus a company can apply 17 per cent of its income tax to fishing businesses whose plans have been approved by SUDEPE (Fisheries Development Authority), 50 per cent to reafforestation and varying percentages to cattle-breeding, tourist hotels, certain industries and any other enterprise which has the official stamp of approval under the fiscal incentives scheme. Most money applied in this way has gone to the North and North-east where development was slow and unemployment a problem. Large sums are involved. The Brazilian cigarette company Souza Cruz, for example, pays about £200 million (about US $500 million) income tax annually and the percentage which can be invested through fiscal incentives adds up to a substantial sum of money. For tax-payers to be able to invest a proportion of their tax-payments in this way and hope to receive interest on the money is refreshing and revolutionary. Critics of the scheme maintain that the money could be better applied in other ways and argue that many enterprises set up by means of fiscal incentives tax-money are ones which would not be economically viable in straight commercial competition.

The total federal revenue in 1970 was 29,819 million cruzeiros of which 4,897 million came from income tax. Income tax revenue in 1961 was only 83 million cruzeiros whereas in 1971 it had grown to 6,353 million.

POLICE

Each state has its own police force responsible for normal police work within that state. State military police forces work closely with their state security secretariats on criminal investigation. They are not part of the armed forces proper but are uniformed police forces with power over all ordinary citizens but with an internal organisation of a paramilitary nature. They deal with riots and are also responsible for the fire services which are organised under the authority of the commanding officer of the military police.

There is also a Department of Federal Police, with headquarters in Brasilia, which was reorganised under Law No 4,483 of 16 November 1964. The federal police are responsible for the supervision of maritime, air and frontier police services, control of land and seaboard frontiers, and for the investigation, in co-operation with the competent organisation of the Ministry of Finance and state authorities, of illegal acts practised to the detriment of the property, services or interests of Brazil. In collaboration with state authorities they investigate crimes which, by their nature, type or scale, come outside the sphere of a particular state, or which Brazil has undertaken by international treaty or agreement to suppress. They are responsible for the investigation, in collaboration with state authorities, of crimes practised against federal agents in the exercise of their duties; and for measures designed to assure the safety of the president of the republic, diplomats, official foreign visitors and Brazilian authorities on official missions. The federal police also deal with censorship of public entertainment (especially films), the co-ordination within the whole country of civil and criminal dactylographic services, the training and specialisation of their own personnel and of state police forces when requested, policing of federal highways, co-operation in Brazil with police services concerned with international or interstate crimes, smuggling and embezzlement, fiscal investigations and investigations of crimes against Indians in close collaboration with the service responsible for their protection. The federal police training-school is the National Police Academy in Brasilia. Brazilian police, including those controlling traffic, carry arms.

JUSTICE

Brazil's judicial system is of the 'continental' type. As a country colonised by Portugal it was only natural that Brazil should inherit the Portuguese legal system of written and classified law and adopt a processual system which still follows traditional lines today, although naturally it has been brought up to date. It is based on civil, commercial, labour, tributary, etc laws, but the interpretation of these follows liberal concepts laid down in the main by the higher tribunals. The system is complex, as in any federation where states have common law for deciding their own individual controversies and where federal justice deals not only with questions of federal power but also with exclusive labour, military and electoral matters.

Cases are heard by a single judge in the first instance, with appeal allowed to tribunals or chambers of tribunals made up of three or more judges depending on the system existing in a particular state.

At the head of the system is the Supreme Federal Tribunal whose function is to preserve the unity of federal law and the supremacy of the federal constitution over any act of government. It also examines requests for extradition and judges complaints made against the president of the republic. Judges serving on the Supreme Federal Tribunal are appointed for life.

In common law the principle of constitutional law overrides everything, including the constitutions of the states.

The system is very different from the Anglo-Saxon system of Britain and the USA. For instance, there are no lively exchanges in court, since cross-examination by the prosecution or defence counsel has to be channelled through the judge. And it is the judge who interrogates the accused and the witnesses before the case is heard in court.

In 1969 a total of 52,436 police arrests were carried out. In the same year there were 28,538 people in prison of whom 812 were women. Of the total of 15,524 individuals who received prison sentences in 1969, 3,216 were sentenced to six months or less and seventy-eight to between twenty-five and thirty years. Nearly a quarter of those in prison during 1969 had been found guilty of homicide. In 1970 there was one case of extradition and fourteen foreigners were expelled from the country.

THE ARMED FORCES

Military service is compulsory for a period of ten months from the age of eighteen and liability for call-up continues to the age of forty-five.

The peacetime strength of the federal forces is about 240,000 men of whom 150,000 are army, 55,000 navy and 35,000 air force. More than half the army strength consists of men doing military service. There is a large immediate reserve.

The Brazilian navy, which is modelled on the lines of the

View of São Paulo, fastest growing city in the world, with over 6 million inhabitants. It is the biggest industrial city in South America. Traffic jams have become a problem in spite of new roads, highways, viaducts and tunnels

The ultra-modern cathedral in Brasilia. Its curved columns represent the states of Brazil holding aloft the Cross of Christ

British, consists of 1 aircraft carrier (ex-British), 2 cruisers, 18 destroyers and escorts, 4 minesweepers, 6 survey vessels, 10 corvettes (tugs), 4 naval transports and 2 submarines. A further 2 submarines of the Oberon class were ordered from Britain, the first entering service with the Brazilian navy in 1972 and the other in 1973. Brazil also added to her fleet by the purchase at about the same time of 6 frigates from Britain, and subsequently more submarines from the USA. Roughly one-fifth of the navy strength is made up by the marine corps. The air force has about 1,500 aircrew and some 600 aircraft and is the largest in South America. Gloster Meteors were bought from Britain after World War II but now the air force is being equipped with French Mirage fighters. A Brazilian-designed trainer is being produced and Italian Macchi trainers are built under licence. The rest of the air force aircraft is mainly of American design.

The Brazilian armed forces are very conscious of the civic role they can play in the development of the country in addition to fulfilling their conventional military responsibilities, and indeed nearly one-third of their budget is allocated for non-military purposes. The valuable civic tasks they perform include the building of bridges, roads, housing estates, drainage and

---

A sugar-cane plantation. Ox carts are still used on many estates for carrying the cane to the refinery

Paddle steamers on the river São Francisco. A good stock of firewood is carried to feed the boilers. There is accommodation for passengers wishing to make the scheduled river journey which lasts several days

F

water systems, dams, wells, telegraph lines and medical posts. In isolated frontier areas, especially in Amazonia, their garrisons provide not only protection but also medical, agricultural and other aid to the local inhabitants.

The Brazilian air force does a magnificent job of keeping communications open to isolated settlements by operating the CAN (National Air Mail) which was originally started in 1937 as the Military Air Mail. Routine flights are operated over immense distances carrying people, livestock, mail and supplies to remote landing-strips in places which are difficult to reach by other means; evacuating sick Indians and settlers alike to hospital when required; and generally giving a kind of aerial 'universal aunts' service to the backlands. The Catalina amphibian, called 'space angel' or 'broody duck' by the locals, has done as heroic work in the Amazon area as the Douglas C-47 in other parts of the country and recently the Buffalo aircraft came to join their gallant ranks. Aircrews never know what to expect but, whatever the given situation in the wilds, the Brazilian air force has a high reputation for being equal to it. They may be called upon to fly out a settler with an arrow through his neck or an Indian with convulsions, or to mount a widescale search for an aircraft which has crashed in some inhospitable part of the jungle.

Brazil is divided into several air zones, each with its command headquarters and defined area of operations. The vast territory of the 1st Air Zone, which has its headquarters in Belém, covers the states of Acre, Amazonas and Pará and the territories of Amapa, Rondonia and Roraima. It is equivalent in size to 44 per cent of Brazil's total area, two-fifths of South America and one-twentieth of the earth's land surface. It also embraces 6,875 miles of frontier bordering seven countries and 750 miles of seaboard.

To cover this area the Brazilian air force operates a dozen C-47s and eight Catalina amphibians on routine flights over regular routes carrying service personnel, nuns and priests, doctors, dentists, supplies, mail, livestock, medicines, equipment and anything else that is needed in remote settlements where aeroplanes have become commonplace but cars may never have been seen. During 1972 the 1st Air Transport Squadron, which serves the area, flew 1,298,581 miles, completed just under 11,000 flying hours and carried nearly 1,125 tons of freight and about 12 tons of mail, as well as 10,165 service personnel and 26,227 civilian passengers. Mercy missions flown by the Brazilian air force in the area save sick or injured people at an average rate of one a day. In addition, air force doctors, dentists and other personnel care for the health and well-being of many tribes of Indians in the 1st Air Zone area at places where the National Indian Foundation has no posts. The air force even flew a herd of buffalo to the Tiriyó Indian village close to the frontier with Surinam, to help the tribe produce meat and milk.

4

How They Live

THE lack of housing became an increasingly serious problem in Brazil due to such factors as a high rate of population growth, the migration of rural dwellers to urban areas and industrialisation. A high rate of inflation also aggravated the situation by making the habit of saving more difficult and less attractive.

Efforts of official organisations dealing with housing during the twenty-five years between 1938 and 1963 were insufficient to meet requirements and in this whole period only 120,000 units were built. The government which came to power in 1964 had to face the problem of a housing deficit estimated at 7 million houses and, in order to meet it, it decided to create both the National Housing Plan (PNH) and also the National Housing Bank (BNH) as an agency of the Ministry of the Interior to carry out the housing policy of the federal government. The resources of the National Housing Bank come from two main sources which it administers: the Length of Service Guarantee Fund (FGTS) and the Brazilian Savings and Loan System (SBPE). The FGTS is made up by a contribution equal to 8 per cent of the monthly salary of every person employed under the system of the Consolidated Labour Laws and provides allowances for unemployment periods, illness and retirement, besides providing financial assistance for house acquisition. The purpose of the SBPE is to channel savings to the housing finance system, at the same time offering prospects of profits to those who invest in its real estate bonds, savings accounts and mortgage bills. Both FGTS and SBPE funds and operations are protected against inflation by monetary correction, which is the quarterly readjustment of operation value in accordance with the fluctuation of general prices.

Complicated though all this may sound, the system has certainly achieved remarkable results. Between its creation in 1964 and 1969 the BNH financed the construction of more than 500,000 housing units; and 127,000 units in 1970. Under the sanitation finance system the BNH also operates through agreements signed with state and municipal governments whereby the water supply and the main drainage systems of more than 280 towns all over the country are being built or enlarged. The BNH planned to spend about £500 million (about US $1,250 million) on the financing of 644,000 new housing units and about £59 million (about US $146 million) on basic sanitation programmes during the period 1971–3.

In a country the size of Brazil, with areas in different stages of development, it is not surprising to find a mixed bag as far as the style of housing is concerned. Dutch, French, Portuguese and other European architectural influences can be seen. There are many charming colonial houses and buildings in Recife, Salvador and also in Ouro Preto, a town about sixty miles from Belo Horizonte which has changed little from an architectural point of view since it was founded in 1711. In the countryside, especially in the states of Rio de Janeiro and São Paulo, can be found huge and graceful old *fazendas* or farmhouses built in an age when six reception rooms and twenty bedrooms were necessary for the owners as well as enormous outbuildings and quarters for their 100 slaves. The walls of some of these mansions, made of mud and stones pounded into place by the slaves, are about 36in thick and provide excellent insulation in all temperatures. There are no old-world, creeper-clad country cottages of the type so cherished in Britain and the USA. Farmworkers and small planters usually live in rather uninteresting little houses, many of which have beaten-earth floors. The house of the humblest squatter is made of mud and wattle with a roof of thin thatch.

European immigrants to the states of Paraná and Santa Catarina built houses characteristic of those in their home countries. Blumenau, as German in appearance as it is in name, is a good example of such outside architectural influence. Some ornate and opulent houses built in Manaus during the rubber boom at the beginning of the twentieth century still stand in the residential area of the city while the opera house, built with imported marble and other materials without regard to expense, is another reminder of the past magnificence of Manaus when world celebrities sang there, racehorses were given champagne and gentlemen sent their shirts to England to be laundered. Palatial though not always attractive residences built in Rio and São Paulo during the coffee boom are tending to disappear and those that remain are often seen rather incongruously cheek by jowl with modern buildings; for building-land in Brazil has increased enormously in value and the tendency in the cities is to demolish the old houses in order that tall blocks of apartments shall take their place. São Paulo, for instance, is a forest of skyscrapers a little frightening in its density. Belo Horizonte is the same but on a smaller scale. Rio, hemmed in on one side by the bay and on the other by mountains, had to grow upwards and did so at a fast pace. The planners have now decided that an entirely new part of the city should be built at Barra da Tijuca which can be reached in fifteen minutes by car over a modern coast road linking it to Rio. A three-bedroomed apartment in one of the modern circular buildings there, on the eleventh floor and with a view to the sea on one side and to the mountains on the other, costs about £18,000 (about US $45,000) payable over seventy months. Rents of apartments in Rio vary between the economical and the astronomical; and an apartment in a fashionable area like Ipanema beach, for example, can cost as much as £500 (about US $1,250) a month unfurnished.

Much has been done to eradicate *favelas* or shanty towns but thousands of people still live in the many that remain. At least in Rio the shanty-town dwellers, the *favelados*, enjoy some of the finest views over the city and bay, although the standard of their housing leaves much to be desired. The authorities often provide alternative accommodation in the form of housing estates or blocks of apartments for the rehousing of *favelados*; but in many cases word of their removal to new quarters brought an influx of new arrivals to take their places in the shanties being evacuated. Since the eager, would-be occupants usually arrived before the old inmates had left, they had to build yet more shanties to house them during the waiting period. The moving of *favelados* can create new problems for them. One contingent was taken to a housing estate so far from Rio that the cost of bus transport and the travelling time involved made it difficult for these ex-*favelados* to go back and forth to their jobs in the city. Latterly the planners have been giving greater thought to the so-called 'urbanisation' of *favelas* whereby the existing shacks are improved while at the same time better sanitation facilities are provided. The conditions of many *favelados* have been made better through the excellent work done by an organisation called *Ação Comunitaria*, which sends teams of professionally trained social workers into shanty towns to advise them on the best ways of community action. A committee is formed to plan and direct operations and a general community spirit is soon established within the *favela*. Everyone sets to with a will to build drains, lay on piped water and carry out other such improvements. The important thing is that the committee is formed of the *favelados* themselves; the *Ação Comunitaria* workers give, not charity, but professional guidance and support. One shanty town of 12,000 inhabitants not far from Rio's international airport has been greatly improved in this way. Here many of the wooden shacks have been reconstructed of brick, drains have been put in, a church has been built and a school installed, all work which has been done by the *favelados* themselves. There is a well-stocked self-service store with a monthly turnover of £12,000 (about US $30,000), a figure which represents £1 (about US $2·5) per month for each man, woman and child living in that particular *favela*. There are other less prosperous shanty towns, however, where living conditions are at a far lower level.

Shacks in the poorer *favelas* are built with considerable ingenuity out of bits of tin, wooden boards from discarded packing crates and any other materials that can be found. Drains and piped water are often non-existent and standards of hygiene can therefore be pitiably low. One blessing at least is the temperate climate in most of Brazil which means that *favelados* are not faced with any problem of trying to keep out the cold. The flimsy shacks clinging precariously to the hills of Rio look as though they would be washed away by the first thunderstorm but in fact they stay put in even the heaviest torrential rain. In some places like Manaus and the *Alagados* of Bahia, the *favelados* live in shacks built on stilts over water and such shanty towns are at least more picturesque and probably healthier than those built in the squelch of low-lying land.

About 500,000 of Rio's population live in *favelas* in and near the city and many of them are relatively prosperous communities, especially those which provided the backbone of samba schools. Many of the samba schools, which are community organisations and centres in themselves, now put on regular shows throughout the year whereas during the old days they appeared only at carnival time. This process of commercialisation has brought regular profits to the samba schools and as a result their members have been able to improve their standard of living quite considerably.

The *favela* of Jacarezinho in Rio is an example of a shanty town which has prospered for different reasons. With close to 100,000 inhabitants in May 1973, its population has tripled since 1960 and it is considered to be a 'city within a city'. This *favela* would confound any visitors expecting to find a settlement of tumbledown shanties inhabited by people in the last stages of misery. It has 20 churches including the largest Roman Catholic church in Rio, 12 small metallurgical industries, 15 shoe-factories, 4 slaughter-houses, several factories making furniture and leather goods, 1,200 commercial establishments, 50 grocer's shops, 6 chemists, 11 poulterers selling 60,000 head of poultry per week, 10 butcher's shops, 30 drapery stores and 6 furniture shops. Altogether it is a going concern and a good example of what can be done to develop an existing *favela in situ* from humble beginnings. Along with six other Rio *favelas* it was brought in May 1973 within the priority urbanisation plan drawn up by the Secretariats of Planning and Social Services which will provide water and drainage.

The social problem of *favelas* was largely created by the migration of country people to the cities in search of riches which in most cases they did not find. This problem is by no means a Brazilian phenomenon: *favelas* under different names exist in other countries and some of them compare unfavourably with those in Brazil. Quick solutions to the problem are not easy to find because they involve not only the need to help existing *favelados* but also the important requirement of keeping rural workers on the land by means of improved labour and living conditions in the countryside.

HOUSEHOLD EQUIPMENT

Virtually all necessary household equipment such as cooking-stoves, refrigerators, air-conditioners, liquefiers and washing machines are now made in Brazil and there is adequate after-sales service for these products. There is no need for domestic heating in houses and apartments except in the southern states where winter weather can be extremely cold. Air-conditioning, rarely found in Brazil not so long ago, is being installed more and more in cities like Rio de Janeiro where the summers are usually hot and sticky. Rooms in houses and apartments are generally air-conditioned by means of individual units fixed in the outside walls rather than by a central system. Cooking in cities and towns is mostly by mains or bottled gas but woodstoves are used extensively in country areas. Charcoal is sometimes used, but not coal or coke. Hot water for domestic purposes is generally obtained through individual gas-heater units even in the majority of apartments in Rio, though central systems are installed in some buildings. Individual electrical units for heating water from showers are used quite extensively;

newcomers tend to view them with some trepidation but in fact they work very well. In the warmer parts of Brazil it is customary to take frequent showers rather than hot baths as they are more refreshing. Where electrical equipment is concerned, it is worth noting that the current in Brasilia is 220 volts whereas in Rio it is 110 volts.

SERVANTS

Domestic help can be found fairly easily, but well-trained servants are not easy to come by. A living-in cook well versed in the culinary arts is a pearl of great price, and indeed her employer will have to pay her a high monthly wage by Brazilian standards of something in the order of the equivalent of £40 (about US $100) per month. Part-time domestic help is available from cleaning women, washerwomen, floor polishers and window cleaners. Very often the janitor of an apartment block or his assistant will take on the job of floor polishing, window cleaning and car washing for a set fee per month. Many of the richer Brazilian families employ butlers or houseboys, and they generally pay their servants lower wages than do foreign residents unused to the local scales and customs.

FOOD AND DRINK

Beans and rice constitute the basic diet of Brazilians throughout the country and most foreigners quickly cultivate a liking for this form of food. If there is one dish that can be considered a national one, as opposed to a regional speciality, then it is *feijoada completa*. This dish can be made in several ways but is always based on beans and rice; and fat pork, pigs' ears, sundried meat and spicy sausage are cooked in the beans. Usually served as accompaniments are such items as *giló* (Indian egg plant); chopped bitter green cabbage; orange slices; manioc flour fried and plain; a hot sauce called *malagueta* made out of red and green peppers; and a mixture of vegetables cooked at the last moment in the beans. Obviously *feijoada completa* imposes a considerable strain on the inside of a man: it is best eaten at lunchtime rather than in the evening and preferably on a day when no pressing engagements are scheduled for the afternoon.

There are many exciting regional dishes such as turtle soup, duck cooked in a special sauce (*pato no tucupi*), lobster or shrimps in coconut sauce, mud crabs baked in their shells (*casquinha de siri*) and excellent sun-dried meat from the North and North-east. It is claimed that *pato no tucupi* is the only true Brazilian dish because it was invented by Brazilian Indians. The story is that they used to roast duck to carry with them as food on their journeys. They found that the duck went bad, however, and after many experiments they hit upon the method of preserving it by pickling it in cassava juice. Considerable African influence on Brazilian cooking is found in the city of Salvador, capital of the state of Bahia, because of the many slaves who were taken there. Some of the favourite Bahian dishes are *moqueca de peixe* of fish done with spices, *xinxim de galinha* made with chicken and *vatapá* which is a delicious concoction prepared from a host of ingredients including fish, shrimps and palm-oil. Typical also of Bahian cooking are the appetisers and sweetmeats sold by amply built ladies at the market and in the streets. Rio Grande do Sul is famous for its barbecued meat and *chimarrao* (mate tea drunk from a gourd). The quality of Brazilian meat has improved immeasurably during the past decade and first-class beef, pork, ham and poultry are now widely available. Unfortunately, lamb is not of the same high standard but in any case it is not a popular meat with Brazilians. Vegetables have also improved enormously in quality and variety, largely due to the efforts of Japanese market-gardeners. Delicious fruit is cornucopian, especially in the North-east. There are super-lative pineapples in the state of Pernambuco as well as the *mangaba* and *graviola* which are used to make unforgettable ice-creams. Housewives in Rio and São Paulo can make their choice from a wide variety of delectable fruits including melons, water-melons, plums, persimmons, mangoes, nesperas, bananas, cashews, grapes, pawpaw and apples. Brazilian strawberries are large and delicious and are obtainable during much of the year.

Many kinds of bread are available, made of wheat, rye or cornflour. Cheese is good and Brazilians enjoy eating it with guava preserve (*goiabada*) as a dessert. The two go so well together that the combination is called 'Romeo and Juliet'.

The poor man's alcoholic drink in Brazil is a fiery white cane rum called *cachaça*, the effects of which can be devastating. Mixed with mashed lemon slices, sugar and ice it becomes the national cocktail called *caipirinha* which finds great favour with foreigners. With lemon juice but without the lemon slices it is a *batida de limão* and this is a very acceptable accompaniment to an outdoor *churrasco* or barbecue. The *batida* is also made with apple, cashew or passion-fruit juice and even with quail's eggs.

Brazilian beer is uniformly good and Brazilians enjoy drinking it, as is shown by the fact that the country's production in the first quarter of 1971 was 440 million litres of bottled and 34 million litres of draught beer worth nearly £20 million (about US $50 million).

Soft drinks are consumed in enormous quantities and production is estimated at 2·8 billion litres a year. Even so, producers have a hard job meeting demands during a particularly hot summer. There are good mineral waters, both fizzy and still.

Scotch whisky has become a very popular drink in Brazil; prices of imported brands are high in the shops but a trifle less so if obtained from a reliable *contrabandista*. Considerable quantities of imitation Scotch whisky have been made in Brazil and the story has it that the very first brand put on the market gave away its false origins by being labelled 'Good Old Queen George Whisky'. There are many brands of Brazilian whisky made with malts imported from Scotland, and they are quite good although not really in the same class as the genuine article. Locally made liqueurs are good and the brandies are unexceptionable in their own way. A great deal of wine is produced in the southern states of Brazil where Rio Grande do Sul, with 256 million litres, accounts for 82 per cent of the country's total annual production. No great clarets or hocks are produced, but 8 million litres in the 'fine wine class' are sold without difficulty. The problem is to find a market for huge stocks of ordinary table wine. The Brazilian wine industry faces an even greater crisis now that Chile and Argentina plan to place large quantities of good-quality wine on the Brazilian market, at low prices, under a Latin American Free Trade Association (ALALC) agreement.

HOW THEY SPEND THEIR MONEY

The very size of Brazil and the wide range of family incomes and household expenses within its population make it difficult for any organisation concerned with statistics to compile figures showing, on a nationwide scale, how Brazilians spend their money. A fisherman in the North-east lives and spends differently from an industrial worker in São Paulo; a cowboy in Mato Grosso usually has dried meat and mate tea as his diet whereas a bank-clerk in Rio de Janeiro may buy what he can afford in supermarkets. Cost-of-living indices and household-spending figures tend, therefore, to be compiled on a parochial basis and generally only in the capitals of the more important states. The official minimum salary is a useful yardstick for calculations. This varies from state to state (268·80 cruzeiros in the state of Guanabara in 1972) and is revised periodically by the government in the light of the cost of living.

A survey made by the Getulio Vargas Foundation in Rio in 1966–7 to estimate household expenses in the state of Guanabara, was made among two categories of families: those with a family income of up to four minimum salaries a month and others earning more than this total. Families in the first category (earning up to four minimum salaries a month or about £70 (about US $175) were found to be spending 48·07 per cent of their income on food; 13·11 per cent on housing;

4·32 per cent on clothing; 9·70 per cent on household items; 4·96 per cent on medical attention and hygiene; 11·01 per cent on personal services and 8·83 per cent on public transport. Some of these figures contrast quite sharply with those given for other states. For instance, the comparative percentage spent on food in Pará was 56·42; 25 per cent on housing in São Paulo; and 12·22 on public transport in Rio Grande do Sul. Average household expenditure on food was much higher than in the USA or the UK, in relation to income.

Rents of houses and apartments are often based on so many times the minimum salary, thus providing a neat way for landlords to have their rents increased automatically when the minimum salary goes up to compensate for the increased cost of living. Another system used is for the rent figure to be linked to the annual cost-of-living index produced by the Getulio Vargas Foundation, with a certain minimum increase figure having been established beforehand.

The rate of inflation is a predominant factor affecting any financial deals in Brazil. Running at something like 85 per cent shortly before the revolution of 1964, it has been contained during the past few years at around 20 per cent per annum and is being further reduced. The period of galloping inflation must have been a nightmare for statisticians since it was possible at that time for apples on fruitsellers' barrows to cost more in the afternoon than they did in the morning.

A characteristic of Brazilian inflation in 1971 was the increased cost of certain agricultural products coupled with the scarcity of some due to increased exports or crop shortages. Coffee went up in price owing to a deliberate official policy to eliminate subsidies of this product sold on the home market. Prices of rice and sugar also increased quite sharply. Food prices rose too, because of new product-presentation techniques used by the growing number of supermarkets which have become popular with Brazilians throughout the country. Clothing tended to rise less in price as compared with other products, however, due to mass production and the introduction of synthetic materials.

A great number of Brazilians, especially white-collar workers, have to live on tight budgets and many of them find that periodic increases in salary do not keep pace with rising prices. Except where housing is concerned, loans can be obtained only at high interest rates over a relatively short period. Nevertheless, a desire for material goods coupled with boundless optimism about the future has resulted in a wave of credit purchasing of items like cars, electrical appliances and television sets. To give an idea of the costs involved: a locally made Volkswagen Beetle costs almost £1,200 (about US $3,000); a colour television set about £400 (about US $1,000); and an average-size refrigerator around £80 (about US $200). There seems to be no shortage of buyers for these and other such goods on hire-purchase terms.

Brazilian families are generally very medicine-minded and spend a lot of money at chemists'. Less wealthy people are apt to be very thrifty in many respects but extravagant in others. A survey carried out about ten years ago, in the state of Pernambuco, among sugar-estate workers who had just been given a dramatic increase in pay, revealed that many of them were spending much of their new-found wealth on transistor radios, shoes and whisky. Most Brazilian families cannot afford to buy many luxury items as yet, but their spending-power is increasing and now all goods are becoming available in Brazil.

SOCIAL SECURITY

Notable social-security legislation was introduced during the régime of President Getulio Vargas in the 1930s, but the system was not overhauled and improved until a few years ago. The main medium of social security is the INPS (*Instituto Nacional de Previdencia Social*) which provides for unemployment and sickness benefits as well as pensions. Every employee contributes 8 per cent of his salary every month to the INPS and his employer pays an equal amount, the maximum salary figure on which this can be calculated being ten times the highest official minimum salary (this varies from state to state but in Guanabara in 1973 it was 312 cruzeiros). After making twelve contributions the employee is entitled, in the case of illness, to 70 per cent of the average of the last twelve contribution salaries plus 1 per cent for every twelve contributions, the limit he can receive being 90 per cent of the last twelve months' contribution salaries. After 30 years' service the employee qualifies for 80 per cent of the average of the last 36 contribution salaries, but the first 24 of these are corrected by an increase to compensate for inflation during the last 36 months. For every year over 30 years' service there is an increase of 4 per cent, so that an employee with 35 years' service would receive 100 per cent of the last 36 contribution salaries with the first 24 corrected for inflation. An employee must have contributed for a minimum of 5 years before reaching the age of 65 in order to qualify for a retirement pension. Another benefit which the employee receives is payment every year in December of the thirteenth-month salary which, as its name implies, is a bonus of one month's salary for one year's service or a proportion of it if the employee started work after 1 January.

Employers make an obligatory annual payment to the INPS, based on the payroll of the company, to cover accidents to

---

Students at the Cidade Universitária (University City), Rio de Janeiro. This is a vast building near Rio's international airport of Galeão. Work on it was held up for many years but has now been completed

A chief of the Karajá Indians, who live on the island of Bananal, carries a large turtle taken from the river Araguaia. His head-dress, skirt and ear ornaments are made of colourful feathers

employees both at work and while travelling between their home and place of work.

Another measure, introduced in July 1971, is the Programme of Social Integration which allows employees to participate in the enterprises in which they work through a Participation Fund made up by deposits paid by employers into the National Savings Bank. The Fund is built up from two sources: the first is a proportion of the company's income tax at the rate of 2 per cent for 1971, 3 per cent for 1972 and 5 per cent for 1973 and thereafter. This represents the government's contribution to the Fund. The second is a proportion of the company's sales bills calculated at 0·15 per cent for 1971, 0·25 per cent for 1972, 0·40 per cent for 1973 and 0·50 per cent for 1974 and thereafter. Payments are made into each employee's individual account with the Fund, the amount varying according to salary and length of service. The amounts credited to individual accounts have an annual monetary correction to compensate for inflation, produce an interest of 3 per cent per annum on the corrected deposits and are added to the profits produced by the investment of Fund capital in selected sectors of the national economy. In each year the individual holder of a credit in the Fund is entitled to draw the monetary correction, the interest and any profit

———

The standard bearer and *mestre-sala* of a samba school dance together in the streets of Rio during a carnival parade. Work goes on all year to make the beautiful costumes worn by members of samba schools at the annual event, new ones being produced every year

Followers of Iemanjá, goddess of the sea, cast their offerings to her into the waters on Ipanema beach, Rio, during their annual rituals on New Year's Eve. If the offerings are carried out to sea, then omens for the coming year are favourable

G

earned by his proportion of the Fund. He is allowed to draw his whole share in the Fund in the case of marriage, retirement, incapacity (in the event of his death his dependants are entitled to it) or for the payment of debts relating to the purchase of a home. If the employee leaves one company for another he is entitled to take his share of the Fund with him to his new employers, without loss.

Complicated though it may all sound, this seems to be a fairer and more workable system than that which has been in force for many years to cover indemnity payments to employees in the event of dismissal. Indemnity was based on length of service, but the system was such that paying off an employee with ten or more years of service became expensive enough to be undesirable from the employer's point of view. The logical result was that employers were apt to dismiss employees, however good their work might be, when they were nearing the ten years' service mark. This arrangement for indemnity still exists, but the employee has to opt for the old or for the new system and he usually chooses the latter as being more favourable to him in the long run.

HEALTH SERVICES

Health has always been a problem in Brazil owing to the prevalence of many kinds of diseases, the lack of hygiene and a shortage of doctors. The state of Guanabara has one doctor for every 300 inhabitants but in parts of the interior of the country the proportion falls to one for every 15,000. The average for the whole of Brazil is about one doctor to every 1,763 inhabitants. There are about 50,000 doctors and 8,000 nurses whereas the World Health Organisation standards of one doctor per 1,000 inhabitants and two nurses per doctor would expect a total of 100,000 doctors and double this number of nurses.

The average number of hospital beds for every 1,000 inhabitants of the estimated population in 1968 was 3·6, the lowest individual figure for any state being 0·5 for Maranhão. There are said to be less than two dozen gynaecologists in Amazonas; and in the states of Minas Gerais, Mato Grosso, Ceará and Paraiba there are a great number of municipalities where there is not a single doctor. The fact that life expectation in Brazil, no more than 43·7 years between 1940 and 1950, is estimated to have risen to over 55 is proof of the success attending the improvement in health services and the efficacy of vaccination and other campaigns in the field of preventive medicine. But it compares unfavourably with a figure of 66 for Uruguay and Argentina.

Brazilian medical men are generally extremely good (though fees for private consultation and treatment are high) but they tend to concentrate in the cities where practices are obviously more profitable. It is in the more backward areas that malaria, hepatitis, tuberculosis, Chagas disease, bilharzia, enteritis, worms and tetanus are prevalent and able to take their toll among communities which lack medical assistance. Infectious and parasitical diseases as a result of malnutrition and lack of hygiene account for 40 per cent of all deaths in the country. Infant mortality before the age of one year is as high as 200 out of every 1,000 in some places.

There are some hair-raising statistics about the incidence of disease in Brazil. About 50 million Brazilians are said to suffer from worms, 13 million from Chagas disease, 10 million from bilharzia and 160,000 from leprosy. A very great deal has been done by the authorities to eradicate smallpox and yellow fever and to keep other diseases like malaria at bay, but it is a hard-fought battle.

Hospitals and clinics in the principal cities are as good as can be found anywhere and the standards of medical, surgical and dental attention are high. One of the world's leading plastic surgeons is a Brazilian named Ivo Pitanguy and he will as easily operate for nothing on a poor patient as he will for a fee on some well-known actress. Training courses for nurses are given in Rio de Janeiro at the Ana Nery School of Nursing which was named after a dedicated Brazilian lady who followed closely the example of Florence Nightingale.

Since January 1972 the Golden Cross organisation has been offering a medical insurance scheme in Brazil on the lines of that provided by the BUPA (British United Provident Association). Those paying monthly subscriptions to the organisation are covered immediately for accidents and after six months for hospital and surgical expenses both within Brazil and when travelling abroad. Certain discounts can also be obtained in some cases on the cost of medical consultation, dental treatment and medicines. In 1973 the monthly subscription to the Golden Cross medical scheme to cover a husband and wife was about £7 or just over US $17. Several hospitals run similar schemes. Surgical, medical, dental and hospital expenses in Brazil on a private-patient basis are little different from those in the USA and the UK.

A remarkable feature of Brazil is the number of mediums who, while allegedly possessed by spirits from another world, are able to effect cures which are often considered to be nothing short of miraculous. Their treatment may take the form of prescription or the laying on of hands, but in many cases these mediums have carried out extremely delicate surgical operations without the use of an anaesthetic and with the aid of a razor-blade or a penknife. On many occasions the medium has diagnosed the trouble before the patient has even had an opportunity to describe his symptoms. People who have been operated on claim to have felt no physical pain during the operation, even though this may have been on an eye cataract or in the stomach. So many of these cures have been photographed, filmed and witnessed by sane and sensible people that it is impossible for sceptics to dismiss them as mere charlatanism.

One of the best-known mediums in Brazil was Zé Arigo, who lived in the town of Congonhas do Campo in the state of Minas Gerais. His cures excited such interest in the USA that a group of thirteen American specialists visited Congonhas do Campo in order to see him at work. He was said to receive while in a trance the spirit of a dead Dr Fritz who guided him in his diagnosis, cures and surgical operations. Thousands of people would readily testify to the almost miraculous cures carried out by Zé Arigo, but this feeling was not shared by the Medical Association of Minas Gerais which caused him to be prosecuted for the illegal practice of medicine. He did not lose his following as a result of this, however. Zé Arigo predicted that he would die within a certain time limit and, before the time was up, he was killed in a car crash.

Several other Brazilian mediums continue their supernatural work of healing and curing and one of them, Lourival de Freitas, has achieved considerable renown in London for his cures and operations there. He is credited with having operated successfully on the knee of Garrincha, a famous Brazilian footballer, and with having cured the footballer's son of persistent headaches by operating behind his ear. Publicity has been given to the remarkable case of a journalist who, because of a malignant tumour, was told by his doctors that he had one month to live. In desperation he consulted Seu Sete da Lira, a well-known medium in Rio, whose treatment consisted of sprinkling sugar-cane rum on those parts of the patient's body where the pain was acute. It is claimed that after five weeks the journalist was cured and able to resume a normal life. Such cures are inexplicable by the standards of logic but there are many witnesses to the fact that they have occurred. The mediums use their special powers only for the good of their fellow human beings and never charge fees for their services.

5

How They Work

AFTER the great slump of 1929 the Brazilian economy slid into a general depression. Exports fell from almost £200 million (about US $500 million) to no more than £72 million (about US $180 million) in 1932. Heavy restrictions were imposed on imports which fell to just over £40 million (about US $100 million) in 1932 as against almost £200 million (about US $500 million) in 1930. Brazil then set out on the road to industrialisation as an alternative to importing and with the object of solving its acute foreign exchange difficulties. Considerable strides forward were made in the textile, cement, foodstuffs, metallurgical and chemical industries. The outbreak of World War II created import problems for Brazil but on the other hand its exports of strategic materials increased enormously. Brazil's industrialisation process was hampered by a shortage of both skilled labour and electric-power capacity. Between 1945 and 1946 its exports grew by only 17 per cent while imports increased by 80 per cent.

Beginning in 1957 foreign exchange and trade policy was modified and a heavy surtax on foreign exchange together with government incentives encouraged further industrialisation. Foreign investments soared to unprecedented levels and in 1957 amounted to £142 million (about US $355 million). From 1946 to 1961 Brazilian industry's real value increased by 262 per cent and in the same period steel production and electric-power capacity were trebled. Incentives to industry between

1953 and 1965 caused considerable changes in the order of importance of commodities on the import list, the greatest change being in capital equipment. In 1953 machinery and other related equipment accounted for 36·7 per cent of all Brazilian imports but by 1965 this figure had dropped to 18·2 per cent. Industrial growth led to larger oil and fuel imports, however.

Brazilian industry continues to expand steadily. It is estimated that the volume of physical industrial production increased by 11·1 per cent in 1970 as compared with 10·8 per cent in 1969 and 13·2 per cent in 1968. By Decree No 67,323 of 2 October 1970 a Fund of Modernisation and Reorganisation of Industry was established at the National Economic Development Bank for the purpose of increasing productivity and improving the competitiveness of Brazilian manufactures in foreign markets, the resources of the Fund being obtained both from the budget and from supplementary internal and external sources.

The tremendous expansion of the Brazilian economy which has taken place since the military régime took over power after the revolution of 1964 has been rightly acclaimed as an 'economic miracle'. Referred to in the past as 'the sleeping giant', Brazil is now fully awake and taking gigantic strides towards becoming an economic power of the first importance.

COAL

Brazilian coal reserves are estimated to be 3·17 billion tons and are mainly in the states of Rio Grande do Sul (1·93 billion tons) and Santa Catarina (1·2 billion tons). The states of Paraná and São Paulo have smaller reserves. The quality of the coal varies widely: coal from Rio Grande do Sul and Paraná can be used for generating steam and electricity while that from Santa Catarina is used by steel-mills. Other coal reserves have been found in parts of northern Brazil but they have not yet been fully surveyed.

Brazil mines just over 5 million tons of coal a year. In 1970 the iron and steel industry used 2,235,444 tons and thermo-electric power 1,527,127 tons. Thirty years ago Brazilian railways and ships used almost all the coal the country could produce but in this sector coal has steadily been replaced by oil as a source of power. In 1955 Brazilian railways used more than 800,000 tons of coal but in 1970 this figure had fallen to 32,861 tons. The mining, processing and transportation of coal gives employment to over 20,000 people and the total value in 1969 was more than £8½ million (about US $21·2 million).

SHALE

Brazil has the second largest reserves of shale in the world. They are estimated to be capable of producing 800 billion barrels of oil or thirteen times more than the Kuwait deposits. Exploitation of shale has previously been uneconomic because of the exorbitant operational costs but now Brazilian technicians claim to have achieved a breakthrough in this field by developing a process called 'petrosix'. Brazil first entered the shale business in 1881, when the Baron of Tremembé installed a small factory to process the bituminous rocks on his farm and thereby provide gaslighting for the towns of Taubaté and Pindamonhangaba in the state of São Paulo, before the cities of Rio and São Paulo had such refinements. The enterprise failed in 1892 but the experiment inspired Russian Tsarist technicians to study the problem. Russian technological co-operation with Brazil in this field continues today.

OIL

Oil was first found in Brazil in 1939 and by June 1954 a total of 404 wells had been drilled. By Law No 2,004 of 1954 the Brazilian government was granted a monopoly on prospecting, mining, liquid hydrocarbons and rare gases and the refining of national and imported petroleum (excluding private refineries in operation before 1954) as well as the transport of petroleum and its by-products and derivatives. In the same year a state enterprise called Petrobrás (*Petróleo Brasileiro SA*) was created; the country's first refinery was built; and the National Tanker Fleet was organised. Average daily production in 1954 was 2,700 barrels but by December 1966 this figure had risen to 150,000 barrels a day which covered about 45 per cent of Brazil's consumption at the time.

Between 1956 and 1969 the Petrobrás research and survey programme resulted in the discovery of new deposits which increased reserves by 284 per cent from 301 million to 582·5 million barrels. In December 1970 reserves were estimated to be 857 million barrels. There are also sediments along the whole Brazilian coastline and recent offshore surveys have established a large area suitable for petroleum exploitation.

There are producing oilfields in the states of Bahia, Sergipe and Alagoas. Production of Brazilian crude oil in 1970 amounted to 61 million barrels which met 33·7 per cent of the country's total requirements. The oilfields of Bahia accounted for 49·6 million barrels, those of Sergipe and Alagoas 11·1 million barrels, while offshore beds along the state of Sergipe coastline produced 164,000 barrels. There are 11 refineries in operation of which 5 belong to Petrobrás. Production by private refineries which were already in operation before the state monopoly was established accounts for only 11 per cent of the total refined by Petrobrás. The approximate consumption of petroleum derivates in 1969 was 475,000 barrels. Strenuous efforts are being made by Petrobrás to expand in order to meet increasing consumer demand, but meanwhile Brazil has to import a large amount of crude petroleum. Oil production in 1971 was 62·2 million barrels.

PETROCHEMICALS

A Petrobrás unit called the President Vargas Petroleum Products Complex started producing synthetic rubber in 1962 and is able to export to Latin American countries which are members of ALALC besides meeting domestic demands. The Pernambuco Synthetic Rubber Company, which started operating in 1965, produces synthetic elastomers based upon ethyl alcohol and has an annual capacity of 27,500 tons. An enterprise called Prosint, which was inaugurated in May 1971, has a capacity of 33,000 tons a year of methanol, a volume which exceeds domestic demand. The Bahia Petroleum Products Complex will produce 250 tons a day of urea and 200 tons a day of ammoniac, based on natural gas from the state of Bahia's oilfields.

The state and private companies in the petroleum products industry are expanding in all sectors, from elastomers to synthetic fibres, paints, plastics, detergents, propane, butane, aromatics and other products. The industry employs about 9 per cent of all workers in the manufacturing industries. New projects should provide about 100,000 new job opportunities of which nearly a third will be for specialised manpower.

ELECTRICITY

Brazil's hydroelectric resources are estimated to be able to meet any demand up to 150 million kilowatts. Consumption in 1970 totalled 37,672,695mWh of which 19,345,230mWh were used by industry and 8,405,802mWh by domestic households. The rest was used by trade, commerce, and public facilities. By the end of 1970 Brazil had an installed capacity of 11,405,000 kilowatts, two and a half times greater than that existing in 1960. Plans are in hand to meet the insatiable demand and it is estimated that US $3·6 billion will have been invested in new schemes by 1975.

ATOMIC POWER

A nuclear plant is being installed near Angra dos Reis, about 160 miles south of Rio, under the control and operation of

Eletrobrás (an organisation of the Ministry of Mines and Energy) and the National Commission of Nuclear Energy. It should produce 500,000kWh from 1976 onwards.

OTHER MINERAL RESOURCES

Brazil's reserves of iron-ore are put at 2 billion 12 million tons. Production in 1970 was about 40 million tons as against 9·3 million tons in 1960. Approximately 70 per cent of the 1970 production was exported.

Known reserves of manganese total 100 million tons. Production in 1970 was 1,800,000 tons as against 950,000 tons in 1960. About 88 per cent of the 1970 production was exported.

Reserves of cassiterite (tin) in the territory of Rondonia are estimated at 10 million tons, an amount that exceeds by 2·4 million tons all known reserves of this mineral in the world. It is expected that mineral riches will be found in the areas through which the transamazonian and the Cuiabá-Santarém highways are being driven. The iron-ore reserves of the Carajás mountains in the south-eastern part of the state of Pará, for example, are believed to contain over 400 million tons.

IRON AND STEEL

Iron and steel production began in Brazil during the sixteenth century with the installation of two mills at Sorocaba, in the present state of São Paulo, for the manufacture of iron. Brazil is now the largest steel producer in Latin America and exports about 10 per cent of its output. Production of steel ingots in 1970 was 5·39 million tons. To meet consumption created by industrial expansion, the Brazilian government established the National Steel Plan which provides for the production of 9 million tons by 1975 and 20 million tons by 1980. This should cover domestic consumption, maintain the rate of exports and provide the necessary reserves to satisfy the market during peak periods. In 1970 there were 33 steel plants in Brazil, 4 rolling mills, 62 producers of pig-iron, and 15 producers of alloy iron. Three state enterprises are responsible for more than half of Brazil's total steel production. In 1969 there were 79,192 people employed in the steel industry.

CEMENT

Brazil is among the thirteen largest producers of cement in the world but its production does not compare with that of the USA, for instance, which has exceeded the level of 60 million tons a year. In 1970 Brazil produced 9 million tons of which the states of Minas Gerais and São Paulo, the biggest producers, together accounted for 4·9 million tons. As regards consumption, in 1970 the states of São Paulo and Guanabara accounted for 4·4 million tons, practically half of the country's total production.

MOTOR VEHICLES

Brazil is the biggest producer of motor vehicles in Latin America, with a production in 1970 of 416,394 units of which 250,289 were motor-cars. In 1969 Brazil ranked eighth among the world's chief producers. Ford, Chrysler and General Motors make cars in Brazil, but the largest share of the market goes to Volkswagen which produced 233,591 units in 1970. Most of the buses are made by Mercedes Benz.

SHIPBUILDING

There are thirty-five shipbuilding and repair yards which provide direct employment for 15,000 people and indirect employment for another 45,000. In 1970 nine ships with a total dead weight of 71,650 tons were delivered (ships of less than 200 tons are not included in these figures). Four main shipbuilding yards account for 75 per cent of the productive capacity of the industry and employ 66 per cent of the total labour force in this sector. At present ships of up to 30,000 tons can be built but expansion plans are under way to permit ships of up to 400,000 tons to be constructed. Brazil has already exported cargo ships to Mexico and a floating dock to Trinidad.

Shipbuilding is an old established industry in Brazil. The building of steamships was started by the Baron of Mauá for use by the Brazilian navy in operations against Paraguay during the war of 1865–70.

AIRCRAFT

The Brazilian aircraft industry existed on a small scale and a precarious basis until 1970 when the government formed an enterprise called Embraer (*Empresa Brasileira de Aeronautica*) which operates under the jurisdiction of the Ministry of Aviation. A minimum 51 per cent of the company's ordinary shares must be held by the government, the rest being held by private enterprise through fiscal incentives. A twin turbo-prop executive/trainer aircraft called the Bandeirante is being built and also a twenty-five-passenger twin turbo-prop aircraft called the Maraba.

APPRENTICE TRAINING

The growing demand by industry for skilled labour has meant that the number of technical training schools has had to be increased and their courses of instruction brought up to date. In 1942 the National Industrial Apprenticeship Service (SENAI) was founded for the purpose of organising and running technical schools for minors and special courses for industrial workers. A similar organisation for training apprentices in business was founded in 1946. Both organisations are funded by industry and trade.

AGRICULTURE

In 1967 there were 3,756,948 rural properties in Brazil covering a total area of 963,563,190 acres and of these 2,848,050 were small farms. In spite of its industrial expansion, Brazil continues to be predominantly agricultural. Productivity varies greatly throughout the country, however, due to different soil quality, climate and farming methods. The yield of rice in Rio Grande do Sul is three times greater per acre than it is in the Northern state of Maranhão. One acre of maize in the state of São Paulo or Paraná yields more than twice as much as does one acre in the North-eastern state of Ceará. Agricultural production is concentrated mainly in the Southern and South-western areas of Brazil where nearly a third of the agricultural land area is used for this purpose. In the North-east less than 10 per cent of the total agricultural land area is developed for agricultural purposes. In the North and North-eastern states, however, there are still the traditional crops of cocoa, rubber, black pepper, sisal, jute, cotton and sugar. But cotton- and sugar-growers of the North-east face stiff competition from the South where the states of São Paulo and Paraná account for 54·9 per cent of Brazil's total cotton production and São Paulo, Minas Gerais and Rio de Janeiro produce 60·3 per cent of the whole country's sugar-cane. Central and Southern areas of the country produce 90 per cent of the coffee, more than 70 per cent of the maize, more than 60 per cent of the rice and about 90 per cent of the soya bean and wheat. Brazil is the second biggest producer of maize in the world. The 1970 crop was 15,381,361 tons of which 1,470,618 tons were exported to the value of £32¼ million (about US $80,596,000).

Traditionally coffee is Brazil's largest single export and its revenue in 1970 was the highest in the last thirteen years. The increase in revenue was due to higher international prices, however, and not to greater production which in fact went down from 37,776,000 bags in 1965–6 to 14,248,000 in 1969–70.

Measures have been taken in recent years to avoid over-production of coffee by eradicating about 1·7 billion older trees, and this has left large areas of land available for diversification of agriculture. At the same time new coffee-trees of high productivity have been planted and more efficient cultivation methods introduced. Basically the policy is still to produce a lot of coffee but from less land.

Brazil is the world's biggest producer of bananas and exports them as well as pineapples and oranges. During the last twenty years great progress has been made in growing other types of fruit such as peaches, strawberries and grapes. Greater attention is now being paid to the planting and industrialisation of fruit in the North-east with a view to export.

With an estimated 97,864,000 head of cattle in 1970, more than one animal for each member of the population, Brazil has one of the four largest herds in the world. Cattle-raising is on the increase as new grazing-lands are developed and, with the present rate of expansion in this sector, it seems likely that Brazil can soon become the largest cattle-producing country in the world with meat as one of its most important exports. Minas Gerais has the biggest cattle-herd of any Brazilian state, with more than 20 per cent of the country's total number of head. Several European breeds are kept where the climate and pasture conditions are suitable, but in most parts of the country the cattle are humped *zebú* which are descended from Brahmin cattle brought originally from India. Dairying is not such a thriving business as is meat production, even though there are about 12 million milk cows in Brazil. Milk production increased by less than 4 per cent during the last ten years and the population's daily consumption per capita remains very low. Among other livestock, Brazil has 66,374,000 pigs; 24,727,000 sheep; 14,609,000 goats; and 16,859,000 horses, asses and mules. There is widescale poultry-breeding and the production of hen eggs, for example, was about 800,000,000 dozen in 1970.

The long-held theory that Brazilian soil is unsuitable for growing wheat has been contradicted by the fact that Brazil now produces enough to meet 42 per cent of the country's demand. Production in 1970 was a record 1·8 million tons, all but a tenth of it grown in Rio Grande do Sul.

FISHERIES

Since February 1962 the development of the fishing industry has been supervised by SUDEPE (*Superintendencia do Desenvolvimento da Pesca*) or Fisheries Development Authority. Fishing companies are exempt from profits tax when their projects have the approval of SUDEPE. This approval also exempts them from paying import duty and industrial products tax on the importation of equipment other than machinery and fishing-vessels that have locally produced equivalents.

Consumption of fish in Brazil of 5kg (about 11lb) per capita per year is one of the lowest in the world, but improved fishing and marketing methods should gradually make fish a more regular item on Brazilian menus than it is at present in family households.

The total catch, including shellfish, was 413,000 tons in 1962. The figure dropped to just over 333,000 tons in 1964, but since then the annual catch has been slowly increasing and in 1969 it totalled about 500,000 tons. Brazil has valuable exports of lobster and shrimp, caught mainly in its north and north-eastern waters. Catfish and red snapper are also exported.

FORESTRY

Much of Brazilian territory is under timber and indeed the country has the largest reserves of hardwood in the world. In Brazilian Amazonia are the world's biggest unexploited forest reserves covering over 1 million square miles. In Southern Brazil, however, reserves of the native Paraná pine, the country's most important source of softwood for its home market and also for export—worth £27 million (about US $67,565,000) in 1970—are becoming exhausted. The Brazilian Forestry

Development Institute has begun massive afforestation programmes, but it will be a race against time to replace the dwind-
ling Paraná pine reserves with planted trees. The planting of
eucalyptus trees was started in Brazil many years ago, mainly to
supply wood-burning railway locomotives with firewood, and
by now the country has more eucalyptus than does Australia.
There continues to be a great deal of predatory cutting of timber
in Brazil, but the authorities are trying to impose long-overdue
controls.

Brazil's main forestry products in 1970 were babassu nuts
(181,000 tons); natural rubber (52,000 tons); mate tea
(113,000 tons); Brazil nuts (104,000 tons) and carnauba wax
(20,000 tons).

TRADE UNIONS

There were 6,138 labour-union organisations existing in
Brazil at 31 March 1972, according to official figures. This total
was made up by 13 confederations, 227 federations and 5,898
unions. Of these 2 confederations, 38 federations and 2,539
unions were rural. São Paulo has the greatest number of
labour-union organisations of any state.

FOREIGN TRADE

Brazil's foreign trade in 1970 totalled £2,200 million (about
US $5·5 billion) which represented an increase of 22 per cent
over 1969. Exports of manufactures in 1970 increased by 58·2
per cent to a total of £182 million (about US $455 million) and
accounted for over 16·6 per cent of the total exports as compared
with 12·2 per cent in 1969. In 1971 they reached a total of
£240 million (about US $600 million), representing 20 per cent
of Brazil's foreign exchange credits. Imports of machinery
and equipment were over £400 million (about US $1 billion)
in 1970. Total freights were £280 million (about US $700
million) in 1970 of which £270 million (about US $674·7

H

million) were maritime, and these figures showed an increase of 26·7 per cent over 1969. Exports increased by 18·5 per cent to £1,096 million (about US $2,739 million) in 1970. At this rate the figure of £2,000 million (about US $5 billion) should be reached within the next four years. The share of coffee in Brazil's total exports fell from 41 per cent in 1969 to 30 per cent in 1971, but the decrease was made up for by the growth in value due to the improvement in international prices.

The USA continued to be the major buyer of Brazilian products with a share of 24·68 per cent in the 1970 total, a smaller percentage compared with 1969 chiefly because of the decrease in its purchase of steel products. However, the USA was still the chief importer of the item 'food and drink products' mainly because of its instant-coffee imports which were 41 per cent (43,000 bags) of the 1970 total Brazilian export of this product—1,041,000 bags at £17 (about US $42·50) each.

Exports to the European Free Trade Association accounted for 12·85 per cent of the total exports for 1970 and those to the Latin American Free Trade Association (ALALC) for 11·07 per cent of the total, half of these being made up by manufactures. Trade with COMECON showed a reduction of 3·4 per cent over 1969 levels. Trade with Canada and Spain has increased considerably and that with Japan has grown by 285 per cent in five years. Brazil does brisk trade with the European Common Market which had a 28·13 per cent share of its total exports in 1970.

Exports to the UK represented 4·8 per cent of Brazil's total in 1970. Britain's exports to Brazil in 1971 were well over £80 million (about US $200 million), a significant increase of more than 40 per cent compared with 1970. Investment possibilities in Brazil are rapidly awakening interest in Britain, especially as regards joint ventures. This recrudescence of interest has come after a long period of stagnancy in Anglo-Brazilian trading relations dating from the time of World War II. Before that and throughout Brazilian history, Britain has enjoyed an extremely favourable commercial relationship with Brazil and there have never been any really serious political issues between the two countries to upset this friendly association. Much of Brazil's development was due to British initiative and capital, especially where public utility companies were concerned. The São Paulo railway, for instance, was built by the British in the 1860s and opened up a rail lifeline for the carriage of passengers and goods between São Paulo and the port of Santos. Its stretch of track built with ingenuity down a 2,000ft high mountainside, is considered to be one of the outstanding engineering feats of the world.

British merchants established themselves in the main ports and cities while traders carried samples of their wares to places off the beaten track. British machinery often had to be delivered on muleback in the earlier days. One enterprising Englishman bought jaborandi leaves in the state of Piauí and shipped bundles of them regularly to Britain where, so it is said, they formed the basis of an anti-baldness lotion sold by a leading firm of chemists. The leaves are now shipped to Israel where they are made into an eye-lotion. British products from textile machinery to Twyfords ware could be found in Brazil and British goods enjoyed a high reputation for quality, happily a reputation that still exists today.

It was not just Britain's difficult situation during and after World War II that brought about the stagnancy in trade between the two countries. It was only natural and logical that public utility companies should be taken over and run by the Brazilians themselves in the course of time. It was equally obvious that, with its increasing industrial development, Brazil would no longer need to buy from abroad many products which it was now making at home. Gone are the days in Brazil when an imported article was nearly always bought in preference to the nationally made one, for reasons of quality. In any case the foreign product, if it has a Brazilian-made equivalent, will nowadays attract such an import tariff that it usually cannot compete in price. Foreign products are of course still sold to Brazil but the emphasis of foreign commercial interest in the country is tending to shift more to the fields of investment, provision of know-how and joint ventures.

The following are the official figures for Brazil's foreign trade in 1971 and 1972:

Exports	*1971*	*1972*
Basic products (value in US $ millions)	1,988·4	2,727·0
Coffee-beans	772·5	1,000·0
Iron-ore	237·3	230·0
Sugar	153·0	421·5
Cotton	137·1	190·8
Soya bean, bran and cake	105·8	277·0
Meat (fresh, chilled and frozen)	98·7	153·5
Others	484·0	454·2
Industrialised products (total)	821·9	1,200·0
Semi-manufactures	240·6	307·0
Manufactures	581·3	893·0
Others	93·6	63·0
Total	2,903·9	3,990·0

Imports	*1971*	*1972*
Live animals, animal and vegetable products (total)	279·6	309·9
Wheat	106·8	113·1
Others	172·8	196·8
Industrial food products, drinks, alcoholic liquids, vinegar, tobacco	15·4	19·7
Mineral products (total)	406·1	499·4
Petroleum (crude oil)	250·6	312·4
Others	155·5	187·0
Industrial chemical products, rubber, etc	523·8	714·0
Textile materials and manufactures	56·8	66·6
Common metals and manufactures	430·8	461·8
Machinery and equipment	1,241·3	1,750·1
Others	281·0	402·6
Total	3,234·8	4,224·1

Exports of Brazilian-made shoes grew enormously in three years from £760,000 (about US $1·9 million) in 1969 to £9 million (about US $23 million) in 1971. The USA alone bought £2,800,000 (about US $7 million) worth of Brazilian shoes in 1970 and other customer countries included Bolivia, Canada, Paraguay, Surinam, Switzerland and the UK. This dramatic increase in exports has created a shortage of raw materials even though the export of hides has been reduced.

Firms controlled by foreign capital are responsible for 43 per cent of Brazil's total exports, Brazilian-owned private firms for 42 per cent and state-owned firms for 15 per cent. While giving all possible export incentives to companies at home, the Brazilian authorities are at the same time conducting an increasingly energetic campaign to sell Brazilian products abroad. Branches of the Bank of Brazil are being opened up in other countries and trade fairs and exhibitions are being arranged. There is a general atmosphere of hustle and bustle.

Brazil had a favourable balance of payments of £200 million (about US $500 million) in 1969 and of £100 million (about US $250 million) in 1970. In 1972 the favourable balance of payments was £1,000 million (about US $2·5 billion) while the foreign trade deficit was £92 million (about US $230 million). The country's monetary reserves of £480 million (about US $1·2 billion) in 1971 rose to £1,800 million (about US $4·5 billion) at 31 December 1972.

FINANCE

The Brazilian *Banco Central* was created in 1965 and before that its functions were performed by a group of organisations including the National Treasury and the Superintendency for Money and Credit. As the chief commercial bank, the Bank of Brazil had accumulated over the years the duties of a central bank but not in the sense of being an organisation controlling monetary policy. Paper-money was issued in accordance with needs but not in pursuit of any particular programme or monetary policy.

After Brazil had assumed certain obligations at the Bretton Woods Conference of 1944, from which the creation of the

International Monetary Fund resulted, it became necessary to adapt the role of the Bank of Brazil to postwar needs when inflation in Brazil was becoming serious. In 1945 the Super-intendency for Money and Credit (SUMOC) was founded, to act as a body directly subordinate to the Ministry of Finance for the immediate purpose of exercising control over the monetary market and for preparing the organisation of a central bank. In 1965 SUMOC was turned into the *Banco Central* which is a government organisation responsible for the issue of bank-notes and custodian of the country's reserves.

The Bank of Brazil, which was originally founded by a royal decree of 1808, is a commercial bank in which the government has a 53 per cent stake and the rest of the shares are privately owned. It acts as agent for the federal government as well as being the largest and most important of the commercial banks. Acting as a rural bank and as an integral part of the *Banco Central* system are two other official functions it performs. In addition it acts as financial agent for the National Treasury, carries out the policy of minimum prices for agricultural and livestock products and acquires and finances stocks of export-able goods. It receives deposits made by federal bodies, voluntary ones from financing organisations and those necessary for the formation of limited liability companies. As an agent of the government it finances agriculture, carries out the policy of foreign trade and finances imports and exports.

The entire capital of the *Banco Nacional de Desenvolvimento Económico* (BNDE) is government capital. This bank was formed in 1952 to act as the government's agent in financial operations relating to the re-equipping and promotion of the national economy. Its object is to provide the necessary capital for the execution of works, projects or programmes which have as their aim the installation, re-equipping or amplification of transpor-tation, port and electricity systems, basic industries, agriculture, warehouses, silos, packing-houses and cold-storage plants.

The government owns 70 per cent of the capital of the *Banco do Nordeste do Brasil* (BNB) which was formed in 1952 for the purpose of giving financial assistance to the North-east of Brazil.

It finances not only agricultural activities but also the foundation and development of industries in the region. As financial agent for the Superintendency for the Development of the North-east (SUDENE), it receives funds from outside sources and income-tax investments under the fiscal incentives scheme.

The *Banco de Crédito da Amazonia* (BCA) was founded in 1950 and nearly all its capital is government capital. It replaced the *Banco de Crédito da Borracha* (BCB) and has as its main object the promotion of natural rubber extraction. It also encourages the industrialisation of rubber and finances other products from the area.

The federal government also has a 50 per cent stake in the *Banco Nacional de Crédito Cooperativo* (BNCC) which was founded in 1951 for the main purpose of giving financial assistance to cooperatives.

Official figures show that at the end of 1970 there were 172 banks and financial institutions in Brazil with 7,682 branches of which more than 70 per cent were private.

Brazil's gold reserves stood at 40,154kg from 1966 to 1970. In 1961 they were 253,200 and in 1964 81,001kg.

Investment banks have been doing well and the main feature of their business in 1970 was a remarkable increase of 127 per cent in fixed-term deposits. These banks also handle a large flow of money invested in government-sponsored projects under the fiscal incentives scheme.

After a long period of stagnancy the Brazilian stock market began to move in 1970 and the index at the Rio de Janeiro Stock Exchange for that year showed an overall increase of 95 per cent over 1969. Stocks of mining, iron and steel, and state banks were those in greatest demand. During the first six months of 1971 the stock market reached dizzy though unrealistic heights, and during the boom period many Brazilians sold property in order to invest in shares. Several people made a great deal of money but when the crash came many skeletons were left on the beach. Since then the securities market has settled to a realistic level where investors can expect reasonable returns over a period rather than spectacular profits overnight.

6

How They Learn

UNDER the Brazilian constitution elementary education is compulsory and free for children from the age of seven to fourteen years. It is estimated that the average rate of attendance at the country's 145,000 elementary schools is 70 per cent and that about 14 million children are enrolled in these schools. This means that between 3 and 5 million children, by not attending school, are helping to increase the already large number of illiterates. The attendance percentage varies greatly from a claimed 100 per cent in Rio and São Paulo to about 40 per cent in some of the poorer North and North-eastern parts of the country. Distance and a scattered population understandably affect attendance in certain areas. On Amazonian rivers, for example, children may have to row for three or four hours to get to school. A large percentage of elementary schools, especially those in the backlands, still belong to the so-called 'school of one teacher' type where children of different ages and grades are taught in a single room at the same time by one teacher. Other inadequacies in the educational system are caused by the fact that many teachers in public and private schools are poorly trained. Nevertheless, many of them deserve the highest praise for doing the best they can in places where city-trained teachers are usually reluctant to live and work.

There is a disturbingly high desertion rate of pupils who leave school for one reason or another. Very often parents, particularly among the poorer classes, take their children away from school as soon as they can read and write because they think that this is enough and, especially in the case of small planters or farmers, because they need extra hands to help with the family work. The Basic Directives for Education Act of 1961 foresaw the need to make school hours compatible with harvesting time, but it has not been successful in this endeavour.

Much is being done by the Brazilian authorities to improve and expand the educational system. The Ministry of Education planned to spend £40 million (US $100 million) in 1971 on elementary education to reach 80 per cent of school enrolment by 1972 and to have 16,440,000 children attending elementary schools by 1973. Under a constitutional amendment of 1969, state or federal governments are authorised to intervene in the administration of any municipality which does not appropriate at least 20 per cent of its income from municipal taxes for elementary education.

SECONDARY EDUCATION

Where intermediate level education is concerned, there were in 1972 11,387 establishments with a total of 5,588,583 pupils. Up to 1965 nearly three-quarters of the secondary schools were private and so, with a limited number of vacancies in public high schools, the poorer classes had difficulty in obtaining secondary education. Great efforts by the authorities have caused this situation to be changed, not only through the provision of more high schools but also by means of grants. A pupil is entitled to a grant only when the income of his parents, divided by the number of dependants, does not exceed the official 'minimum salary'. Funds are made available to state governments in order that they can give such grants in their areas of jurisdiction.

A major reformulation of secondary educational policy is being carried out with emphasis on the creation of comprehensive high schools directed towards the working youth of Brazil. Instead of providing purely academic education, these establishments give professional training so that students can acquire 'marketable skills' which will enable them to obtain profitable employment later. In collaboration with the United States Agency for International Development (USAID) nearly 300 of these schools are being created in the states of Rio Grande do Sul, Bahia, Minas Gerais and Espírito Santo. Apart from Brazil's contribution, financing by USAID involves almost £13 million (about US $32 million) at 2·5 per cent a year, the loan to be repaid in forty years.

The lack of public schools has been one of the main reasons for the high drop-out rate of 60 per cent between the last grades of elementary schooling and the beginning of the secondary level of education; and this is where a serious bottle-neck still exists. Efforts to overcome this include a change in teaching methods which have been traditionally inclined towards professions of prestige such as medicine, law and engineering. The official aim is to 'create a dynamic equilibrium between quality and the democratisation of education'.

UNIVERSITY EDUCATION

An extensive overhaul of Brazilian higher-level educational facilities has also been taking place. There are sixty-two universities and 550 other institutes providing this level of education in Brazil. There were 431,050 students enrolled in them in 1970 and it is hoped that this number will increase to 580,000 by 1973. The number of universities in Brazil has increased greatly during the past thirty years (in 1940 there were only five) and yet out of 1,000 children who enter the first grade of elementary schools only eleven finish higher-level education, deaths and drop-outs accounting for the rest.

Figures for successful graduation are relatively small. In 1962 107,299 graduate students were in college and 20,000 obtained their degrees. The student body in 1968 numbered 280,000 whereas the output of the universities amounted to no more than 30,103.

A large number of candidates seeking a limited number of vacancies remains a serious problem in Brazilian university education. In the last ten years the demand has grown by 112 per cent from 83,000 to 176,000 but vacancies have increased by only 68 per cent. In 1968 there were 200,000 candidates to fill 90,000 available college places. In 1971 170,000 students entered university, a figure nearly as high as the total number of students in college five years previously. Considerable expansion of higher-level educational facilities has been achieved but it is difficult to keep pace with Brazil's rapidly increasing population. However, in 1971, Brazil was able to reach the proportion of 540 university students per 100,000 inhabitants, a figure bettered in Latin America only by Argentina and Uruguay and one which compares favourably with some European countries.

UNIVERSITY REFORM

A university reform is being carried out by the new Department of University Affairs of the Ministry of Education, with the object of bringing the entire system up to date. Some of the principal aims of this programme are to break up the faculties, establish departments for specific branches of learning, create greater flexibility in the curricula and arrange that sufficient public funds are appropriated to ensure that teachers are given remuneration in exchange for full-time work. Previously many university professors worked part-time because their pay was small and they had to take other jobs to supplement their income. Now their university pay is being increased gradually by 360 per cent. A measure to strengthen authority was introduced by a Presidential Act of February 1969 which punishes with immediate expulsion any student engaged in subversive activity within the university campus. Changes have also been made in regard to payment for higher-level education which before had been free. A constitutional law of 1967 specifies that public teaching will be free only for those who can demonstrate their good sense of learning as well as a lack of sufficient parental income to pay for it. In point of fact the amount in annuities collected from those who cannot prove lack of sufficient income is small, since about 40 per cent of university students belong to the level of family incomes lower than £40 (about US $100) or £60 (about US $150) a month. This measure was at first resisted by many students, not so much because of the money involved but because they felt that this might well be the thin end of the wedge.

PHYSICAL EDUCATION AND SPORT

Physical training and sport was usually neglected in Brazilian schools and universities and indeed it was found in 1969 that only 8 per cent of the university students of that time took part in such activities. The Ministry of Education is making strenuous efforts to change this situation by training instructors and providing facilities for physical training and sport in as many parts of the country as possible. It will probably be many years, though, before anything like the Oxford and Cambridge sporting rivalry is found in Brazilian universities.

THE RONDON PROJECT

There is an excellent scheme in Brazil for university students called the Projeto Rondon (Rondon Project), named after Marshal Cândido Mariano da Silva Rondon (1865–1958) who was one of Brazil's most famous pioneers of the backlands. With the object of improving communications, Rondon and his companions built hundreds of miles of telegraph line through largely unexplored country inhabited by hostile Indians and suffered incredible hardships during the course of this work. Himself part Indian, Rondon became the first head of the Indian Protection Service after it was formed in 1910 and was responsible for founding the Xingú National Park in 1952.

The Rondon Project started in July 1967, when a professor from the university of the state of Guanabara took thirty students to the territory of Rondonia where they worked among remote communities during the long vacation. The experiment was so successful that the Rondon Project was officially founded with full support from the Brazilian authorities. Expeditions by senior students to the backlands have been made on a growing scale and now as many as 5,000 university students take part in a single operation during the long vacation. They are divided up into teams of ten and allotted an area of work which is usually far from their home territory. Transport and lodging are often supplied by the armed forces but almost invariably the students find themselves living under rough conditions. During the operation they work unpaid among local communities, usually miles from civilised comforts, and the help they give can be in the field of medicine, veterinary surgery, agriculture, livestock-breeding, building or dentistry according to their own particular sphere of training. They try to instil a community spirit in order that the work should be carried on by the people themselves after the students leave the area at the end of the operation. To keep the thread of continuity even stronger, more than half a dozen 'advanced campuses' linked to 'mother' universities have been established in less developed areas. Thus the federal university of Rio Grande do Sul has an 'advanced campus' in the territory of Rondônia and the university of Santa Maria (also Rio Grande do Sul) has one in Roraima. An 'advanced campus', which usually consists of nothing but a rudimentary building serving as a headquarters, is manned the whole year round by teams from its 'mother' university, each team of twenty-five people spending one month there.

Apart from bringing help to outlying communities, the Rondon Project brings benefits to the students taking part. They get to know conditions in remote areas and this knowledge can stand them in good stead later on when they become doctors, engineers or captains of industry. Some of them in fact return to work in those particular areas after they are qualified. And since students so often have a marked desire to do something about making the world a better place, they feel a sense of satisfaction at shouldering a rucksack and setting off for the backlands on a 'do-good' mission. In this way students' energies are channelled where they can usefully help their country and their less fortunate fellow-citizens as a satisfying alternative to raising barricades or holding political meetings. The Rondon Project has really shown itself to be a remarkably sensible idea on all counts.

ILLITERACY CAMPAIGN

Illiteracy is now being tackled energetically by an autonomous organisation called MOBRAL (*Movimento Brasileiro de Alfabetização*) which has the status of a foundation. Over a period of five months up to the end of February 1971 MOBRAL was responsible for teaching 508,000 illiterates, mainly in the 12–35 age-group. A proper course of basic instruction is given and it is not enough for an illiterate merely to learn to sign his name. During 1971 MOBRAL received about US $13 million (about £5 million) for its programme made up by funds from the Ministry of Education, 30 per cent of the profits of the National Sports Lottery (football pools) and from other sources including private enterprise. The actual cost to achieve literacy was calculated at £6 (about US $15) per head and part of the cost is defrayed by the communities who are being taught: for instance, by the provision of a place where classes can be held. Federal outlay should not exceed £1.20 (about US $3) per capita. Teaching of adult illiterates in Brazil was started in 1947, mainly by church organisations, and good though somewhat isolated results were achieved in certain parts of the country, especially the North-east, by using radio transmission as the main vehicle of teaching. The experience in this field has been useful to MOBRAL which, with more generous funds available, expects to extend its literacy campaign all over the country.

There are many different figures for the number of illiterates in Brazil. The official Brazilian Institute of Statistics estimates that in 1969 the number of persons over the age of 15 who could not read or write added up to 30 per cent of the population or around 16 million people. By adding half the number of children between the ages of 7 and 14 (probably 9 million) a figure of 25 million is reached for illiterates over the age of 7. More pessimistic estimates put the figure of illiterates over the age of 15 at 28 million. The 1970 census indicated that, in the 14–34 age-group, 9·9 per cent of the urban population was illiterate while in rural areas the figure was as high as 35 per cent. The objectives of MOBRAL's literacy programme for the three-year period 1972–4 are to provide courses for 6 million illiterates and more than 1 million semi-illiterates.

FUNDS FOR EDUCATION

A great deal of money is being spent on education in Brazil. In 1970 the federal government allocated some £112 million (about US $280 million) in its federal budget for this purpose. This was the first time in the history of the republic that the Ministry of Education's appropriation exceeded that of every other department in the federal government. The great effort which the Brazilian authorities are making to improve the system and scope of education is illustrated by the fact that general public spending on education in Brazil during 1971 reached £550 million (about US $1·3 billion), a sum equalling all aid allocated by the USA to Latin America through the various programmes of the Alliance for Progress. It represented nearly 4 per cent of the Brazilian Gross National Product, ranking Brazil favourably with other countries in regard to expenditure on education.

7

How They Get About

Up to a quarter of a century ago the lack of good roads seriously hampered the development of Brazil and caused many inland areas to be virtually inaccessible. There were then less than 1,000 miles of paved roads in the whole country. Anyone travelling in the 1930s between Rio and São Paulo usually went by overnight train or caught a Royal Mail or Blue Star Line ship between Rio and Santos. The car journey over a rough road was an uncomfortable and doubtful undertaking with risks of punctures, breakdowns and broken springs. Motoring on upcountry roads in those days involved clouds of dust in dry weather and the need for chains on the tyres during the rainy season. Beef cattle were often driven 500 miles on the hoof to market because there was no other practical way of getting them there. Trams provided the means of transport for most people living in cities. The Amazon river was the main transport route in the North for river passenger-boats, canoes and Booth Line steamers, while in the South the railways were the main lifelines for the carriage of passengers and freight. In 1930 one could make a three- or four-day journey by train (time often suited the whim of the engine-driver) from São Paulo right across Mato Grosso to Corumbá near the Bolivian frontier over the Noroeste Company's metre-gauge track which is still operated today. But getting about in most places was often difficult and usually tedious.

After World War II the aeroplane had a revolutionary effect on getting about in Brazil, a country which lends itself admirably to air transport because of the distances and the terrain. Air

companies sprang up and operated mainly war-surplus DC-3s,
sometimes on little more than the proverbial wing and a prayer.
Nervous travellers may occasionally have pinned their faith
on the country's old adage that 'God is a Brazilian', but in
point of fact there were remarkably few mishaps. Brazilians
took to air travel and the aeroplane soon became a familiar
sight at places in the interior where bullock carts and rickety
1929 Fords were the usual means of transport. Nowadays
domestic routes are flown with modern aeroplanes all over the
country and a kind of aerial bus service called an 'air bridge'
copes with heavy passenger traffic between Rio, São Paulo,
Belo Horizonte and Brasilia. Air taxi services can be found
almost everywhere.

Modern roads and highways have been built and work on
new ones continues at a fast pace. Hordes of buses roar through
the countryside, in some cases carrying passengers on journeys
lasting two days or more. One can travel over the paved road
from Rio de Janeiro to Campo Grande in Mato Grosso in a
comfortable sleeper bus with hostess and piped music aboard.
The journey, which is about 100 miles longer than the distance
between Land's End and John o'Groats, is covered in nineteen
hours, including stops on the way, and costs each passenger
about £10 (about US $25). The network of good roads has of
course brought out large numbers of heavy lorries which carry
enormous quantities of goods and livestock in all directions.

The railways are making a bid to recapture lost traffic by
putting on modern trains which will be able, for example, to
carry passengers between Rio and São Paulo in a quarter less
time than the buses take at present.

The older ferryboats plying across the bay between Rio and
Niteroi have been supplemented by hydrofoils which do the
crossing in a few minutes. The British-financed Rio-Niteroi
bridge will carry road traffic across its enormous span from one
side of the bay to the other and cut out the long delays previously experienced on the car ferries, especially during weekends and holidays.

It has become nothing out of the ordinary for a tourist or
I

businessman to fly from Rio to Brasilia and back in the same day and yet this is about equivalent to flying from London to Madrid after breakfast and returning in time for dinner the same evening. Getting about in Brazil has certainly become immeasurably easier than it used to be now that the transport system has improved so dramatically.

RAILWAYS

Nearly all the twenty-six railways are owned and run by the State. The total length of track is about 20,000 miles of which some 1,600 are electrified. Approximately 16,000 miles are operated by the *Rede Ferroviario Federal SA*, 3,000 by state governments and no more than 1,000 by private companies. About 90 per cent of all the track is metre gauge, the rest being some 2,000 miles of wide gauge (1·44m and 1·60m) and 140 miles of narrower than metre gauge. The state with easily the longest extent of track is Minas Gerais with 3,000 miles while Acre, Amazonas and Roraima have none at all. Unprofitable track is being closed down in some places and elsewhere lines are being appreciably shortened by the straightening out of unnecessary curves and detours. One popular story to account for the meandering of some Brazilian railway lines is that the original engineers who built the track were paid so much a mile. Another is that influential local dignitaries often persuaded the engineers to take the line through their particular towns or villages even though they did not happen to be on the planned route.

In 1970 there were 1,508 diesel, 597 steam and 246 electric locomotives in service on Brazilian railways with 4,611 passenger and 59,382 freight cars. In that year they carried 332,410,000 passengers, 568,000 tons of livestock, 135,000 tons of baggage and parcels, and 49,666,000 tons of freight. The railways employ about 170,000 people and generally operate at a loss. There are as yet no underground railways operating in Brazil but work on building them has been started in Rio and São

Paulo where it is becoming increasingly difficult to commute between home and work on the surface.

ROADS

In 1970 there was a total of about 650,000 miles of roads open to traffic in Brazil as compared with 209,925 miles in Britain in 1971 and nearly 3 million miles of surfaced roads and streets in the USA. About 31,000 miles of Brazilian roads are paved but the figure is constantly increasing since work on new roads continues all the time. In 1970, for example, about 2,500 miles of paved roads were built as against 1,875 in 1969 and 1,340 in 1968. More than ten years ago the 1,350 mile long Belém–Brasilia highway was built not only as a road link between the South and the most important port in the North but also to open up virgin land beside the road for agricultural development. Now the transamazonian highway, a colossal project costing some £200 million (about US $500 million), is being built right across the north of Brazil from east to west as the backbone of a road system falling within the so-called National Integration Plan. The transamazonian highway, which has become a kind of symbol of Brazil's progress and development, runs roughly parallel to the Amazon river and will link the South Atlantic and Pacific coasts. Another great highway is being built up the centre of Brazil from Cuiabá, capital of the state of Mato Grosso, to Santarem on the Amazon river. These two great roads, cutting through many areas never before explored, will provide a means of reaching and exploiting mineral resources besides making it possible for migrants, mainly from the impoverished North-east, to establish new agricultural settlements with government assistance. They will also open up road communications with and between places on the Amazon river which, like Manaus, could up to now be reached only by water or by air. Some critics of the transamazonian highway maintain that the large-scale cutting down of forest which will follow construction of the road can endanger world oxygen supplies. Others believe that the soil under the forest is poor and incapable of producing more than one or two crops after the land has been cleared of trees. Anthropologists fear that the advent of civilisation to these areas of virgin forest will mean the kiss of death for many Indian tribes. Such considerations will not halt the inexorable bulldozer of development but they may persuade the driver to proceed with caution.

Road traffic is growing all the time and with it the incidence of rush-hour snarl-ups in the big cities. Parking is a problem, especially in Rio where many motorists find no alternative but to leave their cars on the pavement. Parking-meters do not yet exist. Taxis are reasonably cheap but some of them are driven in such ebullient fashion as to test the nerve of even the most courageous of fares. Traffic accidents are a regular feature.

At the end of 1969 there were nearly 3 million licensed motor vehicles in Brazil of which two-thirds were passenger-carrying. Goods vehicles numbered 615,615. During 1969 the 3,735 registered road transport companies carried 4,887,796,242 passengers (São Paulo accounted for nearly one-third of this figure) and 33,252,687 tons of freight.

WATERWAYS

The most important waterways are the Amazon and its tributaries, the Paraná, Paraguay and São Francisco rivers. Every imaginable type of rivercraft operates on the Amazon and every kind of merchandise is carried by them. Canoes and small boats with thatched roofs to keep the cargo protected from the sun bring fruit and vegetables to riverside markets at Manaus. Not far from the centre of the city there is a sort of fluvial bus station where topheavy-looking double-decker river boats are tied up awaiting passengers. Notice-boards on them list the attractive-sounding places they call at on the Amazon. Along the river there are single-deckers and double-deckers, some with chicken-coops on top, others with cattle standing patiently on the lower deck. The most elegant craft are the cargo-carrying *iates* or yachts of different sizes with raked masts and jutting bowsprits. All types of Amazon rivercraft congregate at the *ver-o-peso* (see the weight) market in Belém to provide a boat-fancier's delight.

Fluvial transport along the length of some of Brazil's other great rivers is limited by rapids and waterfalls and it will be road rather than water transport which can lead to development of the areas alongside them.

AIR TRAFFIC

Brazil's first commercial air transport company, *Viação Aérea Rio-Grandense* (VARIG), was started in 1927 with two aeroplanes. It is now the biggest in South America, operating sixty-six aircraft to nineteen countries as well as domestic routes. In 1970 there were three other air companies operating, but in the following year the Brazilian government planned to merge two of them and reduce the total number of companies to three. In 1970 there were 3,718 civil aircraft of all types registered with the Brazilian Department of Civil Aviation as compared with 2,227 twenty years before. During 1970 a total of 3,046,899 passengers embarked and 3,041,746 disembarked at Brazilian airports on domestic and international flights. The addition of passengers carried on private and official flights brought these figures to 3,245,756 and 3,234,395 respectively. More than half the passenger traffic on domestic flights was handled by the city and international airports of Rio and São Paulo as a result of the frequent use by businessmen of the 'air bridge' linking the two cities.

Aircraft used by civil airlines are mainly of American manufacture, the rest being British, French and Japanese types. The DC-3 played an heroic role in the development of Brazil's air passenger and freight services and it was decided only recently that the time had come for this old faithful to be retired with full honours.

The ever increasing cost of air passages is the main problem affecting airline operation. In 1969 VARIG was able to fill only 57 per cent of its passenger and 58 per cent of its freight capacity. Notwithstanding, this and the other Brazilian airline companies have managed to maintain a high standard of efficiency, courtesy and comfort.

8

How They Amuse Themselves

BRAZILIANS are a gay and lighthearted people who work hard but who have a great capacity for enjoying themselves during their leisure time. Business tycoons or clerks, bus-drivers or civil servants, they all try to gain the maximum amusement from the time available at weekends and on holidays. This can take the form of bathing, fishing, golf, weekend cottages, camping, horse racing, family outings, meals in restaurants or relaxation at home. Weekends and holidays are for enjoyment and Brazilians certainly make the most of them. Their great advantage is that the climate generally allows all facilities for enjoyment the whole year round.

The beaches are a never-ending source of pleasure and amusement for Brazilians living within reach of them and especially for Cariocas who make a cult of going to the beach, and, as the Brazilian expression has it, 'falling into the water'. When the weather is fine the beaches of Leme, Copacabana and Ipanema are crowded during weekends and holidays and it is doubtful whether even a revolution or momentous happenings on the world scene would deter the people of Rio from indulging in this healthy and almost ritualistic pastime. Paulistas drive more than thirty miles down to the beaches of Guarujá, near Santos, but often they struggle back in bumper-to-bumper conditions like those found on the London to Brighton road on an English bank-holiday.

The beaches can be enjoyed by only a limited percentage of the population but there are two amusements, football and carnival, which appeal to practically all Brazilians, whether they live near the sea or 1,000 miles away from it.

FOOTBALL

Football was started in Brazil by the British and it grew into such a nationwide sport that today more than 250,000 Brazilians are playing the game, including 6,559 professionals. The Brazilians became superlative players, as they have shown by winning the World Cup three times, and produced one of the greatest footballers of all time, Pelé. He is known to football fans the world over but not all of them would recognise him by his real name which is Edson Arantes do Nascimento. Scorer of 1,000 goals, Pelé has retired with full honours from international football but continues to play for his home team of Santos. Pelé always played and acted like a champion.

Brazilians are passionate football fans and when they set off in cars bedecked with huge flags to support their club team, the journey is not so much a pilgrimage as a crusade. The scoring of a goal causes a volcanic eruption of applause from the team's supporters accompanied by a triumphant waving of those enormous flags while outside the stadium a fusillade of rockets will probably mark the happy occasion. The scoring of a goal for Brazil in a World Cup match will cause such a release of fireworks in Rio that any uninitiated foreign visitor may well imagine that the city is under heavy bombardment. Orderliness and good-humour are qualities of Brazilian football fans, whatever the outcome of the match. It is amazing to see how more than 150,000 people leave the Maracanã stadium in Rio without any pushing or jostling, whatever primeval passions may have been aroused during the game.

Football pools did not exist in Brazil until 1970 when the *Loteria Esportiva* (Sports Lottery) was introduced with full government backing. A large percentage of the take is appropriated by the government and applied to public services, especially education. But the jackpot can still be enormous.

In early May 1972 the single winner in that week won the equivalent of nearly £1 million (about US $2·5 million), a world-record prize at the time for football pools. The *Loteria Esportiva* provides a source of amusement and hope for millions of Brazilians and it has now become a matter of routine for them to try their luck.

CARNIVAL

Carne vale means 'Oh flesh, farewell' and Brazilians certainly celebrate carnival with gusto every year as a way of saying farewell to the flesh. A carnival dance in a country village can be as much fun as the sophisticated kind in cities like Rio, Recife and Florianópolis which enjoy a high reputation for the warmth and verve of their carnival festivities. It was not until the latter end of the nineteenth century that carnival in Brazil became officially respectable, largely due to the influx of Europeans, especially the Portuguese who had a love of this form of enjoyment. Previously the authorities frowned on carnival frolics and in 1865 they banned masked festivities on pain of degradation of whites and public whipping of Negroes and mulattos. After carnival had become accepted as a popular activity, it consisted of a great deal of horseplay. Buckets of water were thrown over merrymakers within range until ᵉmethods were improved and perfumed water in waxen balls shaped like fruit became fashionable. These in turn gave way to small metal squirt-cylinders containing perfumed ethyl-chloride which, though now officially banned, can usually be obtained from streetsellers for a consideration.

Virtually everything stops for carnival while Brazilians give themselves up with joyous abandon to four days of pre-Lenten merrymaking. Carnival balls are organised in theatres and clubs and there is spontaneous dancing in the streets. The colourful parade of samba schools through the *avenidas* of Rio is one of Brazil's biggest carnival attractions. It is a wonderful spectacle as the groups, wearing magnificent costumes and peacock finery, twirl and pirouette past to the irresistible beat of the accompanying music. There is a great deal of good-natured rivalry among the groups for selection by the panel of watching judges as champion samba school of the year. Carnival is the annual joyous safety-valve of the Brazilian people and a period of delirium when all set out to thoroughly enjoy themselves. Foreign visitors usually become infected with the atmosphere of spontaneous gaiety and often find themselves possessed of hitherto unsuspected resources of personal energy to carry them through long periods of sustained merrymaking.

THEATRE AND MUSIC

On the whole Brazilians are not regular theatre-goers but they turn out in force to see visiting productions from abroad of theatre, opera, ballet or concert. Such productions are usually put on in the municipal theatres of Rio and São Paulo. Thanks to a number of small groups, Brazilian theatre has been developing over the past thirty years and there are good artists and good productions. Brazilians are lovers of Shakespeare and have made translations of his works. A notable production of *Macbeth* in Portuguese, for example, was staged at the charming pink-painted Teatro Santa Isabel in Recife. A Recife professor was such an admirer of Shakespeare that he translated all his sonnets into Portuguese and achieved something probably unique by using the Portuguese of Shakespeare's time.

The remarkable *Teatro Amazonas* or Opera House of Manaus, which was built during the rubber boom at the turn of the century with imported marble and without regard to cost, was host to many visiting opera companies from abroad and to some of the most famous artists of the day. That companies should have travelled 1,000 miles up the Amazon in the conditions of those days to give their performances is truly remarkable and one hopes that fees matched the opulence of life in Manaus during that amazing bonanza period. The Opera House has been well preserved but the auditorium is nearly always silent and empty now.

Brazilians have been fortunate enough to see some of the world's greatest artists, including Eleonora Duse in 1885 and Sarah Bernhardt in 1886, 1893 and again in 1895.

The two best-known Brazilian composers have been Carlos Gomes (1836–96), whose *O Guarani* was played in the Scala opera house in Milan in 1870, and Villa-Lôbos (born in Rio on 5 March 1887, died 1959), composer of more than 1,700 works from simple popular melodies for the piano to orchestral compositions.

The Brazilians are an extremely musical people and popular music has always formed an important part of their lives. Some of the first popular musicians were small groups of Negro barbers whose duties also included blood-letting and dentistry. Travellers during the days of slaves recorded the fact in their writings that many *fazendas* (big farms) had their own Negro orchestras. There was great Portuguese as well as African influence on Brazilian popular music and by now there are a bewildering number of types and rhythms like the *modinha*, maxixe, samba, *chôro*, *marcha* and *frevo*. The samba was born in settlements on the hills overlooking Rio and the first one that was composed, called *Pelo Telefone*, swept the country. This was in 1917 and since then Rio has continued to be the birthplace of many beautiful *sambas do morro* (sambas of the hill). The film *Black Orpheus* captured very well the atmosphere of the Rio hill dwellers and their music.

More recently Brazilian popular music became well known abroad through the fine compositions of Vinicius de Morais, especially *The Girl from Ipanema* and through the advent of *bossa nova* (new style). Today there are many talented young composers and players, including the superb guitarist Baden Powell.

Regional music of the North-east became known and loved through the voice and guitar music of Dorival Caymmi, the doyen of Brazilian folk-singers. Fishermen's songs which he collected from the beaches of his native state of Bahia tell plaintive stories of storms, dusky beauties and white sand, of human dramas and *jangadas* which failed to return from fishing.

FILMS

The first Brazilian full-length film, entitled *Os Estranguladores* (*The Stranglers*), was produced in 1906. There is an expanding film industry and several Brazilian films have won international prizes. However, most of the films shown in Brazilian cinemas continue to be foreign productions. The Brazilian film director probably best known by name to British audiences was Di Cavalcanti who directed several good films in Britain during World War II.

There are 3,085 cinemas in Brazil and in 1970 a total of 210 million entrance tickets were sold. The number of cinema attendances has been declining steadily since 1961 because of television competition. On an average Brazilians go to the cinema only 2·3 times a year as compared with a figure of 44 in Britain.

RADIO AND TELEVISION

Radio started in Brazil during the commemorations of the country's hundredth year of independence in 1922 when a small transmitter of 500 watts installed on the Corcovado mountain relayed the president's speech inaugurating the International Exhibition in Rio de Janeiro. It has become one of the most powerful social factors in Brazilian life by providing a means of communication whereby millions of people, educated or illiterate, in cities or remote settlements, can listen to news, sport, music, talks, religious programmes or educational instruction. Every public bar in even the smallest upcountry village has its radio receiver and only four state capitals have less than six transmitting stations. In 1939 there were 64 radio stations in Brazil, but by 1969 this number had grown to 994 of which 300 were sited in state capitals and the federal district. Weekly transmission hours in the same year totalled 108,386·9 with easily the highest percentage being taken up by popular music.

Radio sports commentators in Brazil deserve special mention for their masterly powers of description and their capacity for keeping listeners in a state of agonised excitement even at duller moments when the goalkeeper is merely retrieving the ball from behind the backline. The feeling of suspense is never allowed to slacken and when finally a goal is scored then the commentator inflates his lungs and gives vent to a long-drawn cry of 'Goooooool' ranging from falsetto to the lower octaves. Naturally the cry is more subdued and less enthusiastic when Brazil is playing an international match and the other side scores. Commentators at race meetings are able to pass on a note of tremendous personal excitement to their listeners, but they achieve such a machine-gun rate of words that it is often difficult to understand what is happening, especially when the horses draw near the winning post. Sports commentaries in Brazil are never dull even though the event may be.

Television started in Brazil in 1950 and by 1969 there were fifty-one stations in the whole country, nearly all of them in state capitals. The most powerful is the Marconi-equipped station of the *Jornal do Comércio* newspaper in Recife. The total weekly transmitting hours of all television stations in Brazil during 1969 were 3,136·8, with films having the lion's share of programmes. Considerable attention is being devoted to the field of educational television, because of its obvious potential in a country the size of Brazil. However, it has not achieved much popularity so far.

Nearly all Brazilian radio and television stations are privately owned and operated, mainly by the newspapers. Owners of radio and television sets do not have to take out licences for them or pay any fees.

BOOKS

According to Brazilian official figures published in 1971, there were 352 university, 350 specialised and 1,452 public libraries in 1968 apart from the National Library in Rio.

Brazilians are keen readers and many of the more wealthy

have excellent private libraries. Bookshops are well stocked with national and foreign titles and translations into Portuguese. Several of them stock rare books which command high prices, especially in the case of Brasiliana. Book fairs are held periodically at stalls out of doors in Rio and they attract large numbers of the public.

The publishing trade in Brazil has been growing since 1964, but as yet the issue of a work of fiction does not usually exceed 5,000 copies except in the case of works by best-selling Brazilian authors like Jorge Amado and Érico Veríssimo. A new books policy was introduced in 1970 by the Minister of Education under official decree. This allows the National Book Institute to make agreements with Brazilian publishers for the cash purchase of a certain number of copies of selected titles published by them. By this means a large number of educational books and works of fiction are distributed by the National Book Institute to libraries and schools at a low cost.

MUSEUMS AND ART GALLERIES

There are about twenty-five federal, twenty-five state and twenty municipal museums apart from ecclesiastical and privately owned ones.

There are interesting collections in the museums at the town of Ouro Preto, itself a national monument, and in the charming Gold Museum at nearby Sabará where objects and instruments used in old-time mining days are on view. The Imperial Museum in Petrópolis shows a collection of objects from the time of the Brazilian Empire, including the imperial crown. There are several collections open to the public showing the day-to-day life and art of Brazilian Indians. A wide variety of non-static exhibitions of art are shown by the huge Museum of Modern Art in Rio which also holds courses oi painting, design, interior decoration and painting for children. The well-known *Bienal* (Biannual Exhibition of Modern Art) of São Paulo is held at the Museum of Modern Art in that city and many international artists have shown their work there. The listing and preservation of works, monuments, documents and objects of historical and artistic value in Brazil is carried out by an organisation called the *Patrimônio Histórico e Artístico Nacional.*

In many Brazilian country areas there are traditional dances and musical pageants which have been handed down from early colonial days and they are still performed with undiminished zest today. They usually reflect the influence of religious teaching and Brazilian Indian, African or European culture, although in some cases the result has become a mixture. Later immigrants also brought their dances and customs with them, especially to the South. For instance, maypole dancing and a kind of morris-dance are performed in the state of Santa Catarina.

The gaucho cowboys of Rio Grande do Sul dance the *chula*, a sort of duel to see which of two can improvise the more intricate steps. A long pole on the ground marks the division between the two participants who, wearing riding-boots and enormous spurs, take it in turns to dance, rather in the spirit of 'Anything you can do I can do better'.

In Salvador and Recife the Negroes keep up the *capoeira*, an extraordinary dance which resembles a combination of ballet, gymnastics and ju-jitsu. The two 'antagonists', stripped to the waist, circle each other warily and then one makes a lightning simulated attack on the other. More often than not the attack is delivered with the feet while the owner of them is doing a handstand. Some *capoeira* blows can kill but the dancers are able to judge distance to a nicety in order that targets are missed by a hair's-breadth. The 'dance fight' is accompanied by music usually provided by the *berimbau*, a strange instrument of African origin. It consists of a bow with a gourd attached to one end of the stave and the metal bowstring is played by the musician with a short rod. The *capoeira* was originally intro-

duced by African slaves as an extremely effective means of
attack or self-defence, but it was not allowed as such by the
colonists and therefore became disguised as a dance. In the
early 1800s formidable gangs of *capoeiristas* armed with razors
became a menace and had to be suppressed by the police.

Musical pageants are more gentle affairs and generally the
basic theme they represent is the triumph of good over evil.
In the *congadas*, for example, one group of Negroes dressed in
blue represent the Christians and another group, wearing red,
represent the Moors. To the accompaniment of music provided
by guitars and drums the two groups fight and sing in a mock
battle; the Christians always defeat the Moors who are then
baptised. The united groups end up by holding a celebration
in honour of the black São Benedito, the patron saint of all
Negroes in Brazil.

Another pageant is *bumba-meu-boi* which has an ox (*boi*) as
its central figure. There are regional variations in regard to
the presentation. One actor is dressed up as the ox in a con-
traption of wood and cloth with head and horns attached. The
rest of the participants, in gay costumes, represent Indians,
Negroes and whites. The theme of the pageant is a simple one.
A Negro has stolen and killed an ox belonging to a white man
but the owner saw him do it. Therefore the ox has to be
resuscitated, a task that is performed by the witch-doctor.

During the old days musical pageants were an innocent form
of amusement for slaves in Brazil. As an integral part of Brazilian
folklore they serve no less today as frolics for country people,
few of whom yet have the benefits of cinema, television and other
sophisticated sources of entertainment.

THE PRESS

There are 227 daily and 30 evening newspapers as well as a
large number that come out weekly, twice monthly or irregu-
larly. Some evening papers have their first editions on the news-
stands in the morning and thus fill the news gap on Mondays

when some dailies do not issue. The Brazilian press has always maintained high standards and many newspapers enjoy a well-deserved reputation for their coverage of home and foreign news, accuracy of reporting, objectivity of comment and presentation. Some of the most widely read newspapers are the *Jornal do Brasil, Correio da Manha, O Globo, O Estado de São Paulo* and those belonging to the *Diarios Associados* group of the late Assis Chateaubriand who was well known in Britain when Brazilian Ambassador to the Court of St James. This same group owns the *Correio Braziliense* in Brasilia and the *Diario de Pernambuco* in Recife which is the newspaper with the longest uninterrupted circulation in South America. There are many good provincial newspapers such as the *Folha do Norte* in Belém and the *Correio do Povo* in Porto Alegre. The *Brazil Herald* is the only English-language daily in the country.

A surprising number of different magazines are sold and two of the most popular ones, *Manchete* and *O Cruzeiro*, which both issue weekly, are of excellent quality and produced with very advanced colour-separation techniques.

The Brazilian press is subject to a system of 'autocensorship', laid down by the authorities, whereby rules are established about what should not be published for reasons of national security or on other grounds. Some newspapers, notably *O Estado de São Paulo*, have made no secret of the fact that they find this system irksome and, as a protest, this paper has sometimes come out with cooking recipes in place of the columns it normally devotes to political comment.

The censorship authorities have kept a close eye on pornography and in April 1973 they banned the sale of more than fifty magazines, *Playboy* included, which they considered to be erotic and unsuitable for local reading. One news-seller in São Paulo was quoted as saying that he could not understand the reason for this ban since the magazines in question, being printed in a foreign language, could evidently be bought and read only by members of the 'cultured class'.

Although it may sometimes feel restricted by official rules and regulations, the Brazilian press still retains the capacity to

K

inform and influence its readers. Newspapers are widely read in Brazil and, generally speaking, Brazilians follow the theme of a song from the musical show, *Lock Up Your Daughters*—put on some years ago at the Mermaid Theatre in London—which was: 'It must be true, I read it in the papers, didn't you?'

On the other side of the coin, many Brazilians are irritated by the fact that the foreign press rarely prints anything about Brazil except for subjects of a sensational nature like the genocide of Indians and the alleged torturing of political prisoners.

SPORT AND RECREATION

In 1941 an official organisation called the *Conselho Nacional de Desportos* (National Sports Council) was founded for the purpose of encouraging and supervising the practice of sport in the whole of Brazil. Now linked in an advisory capacity to the Ministry of Education and Culture, the CND disposes of official funds and a percentage of the proceeds from the football pools to give financial assistance to a large number of sports confederations and associations. There are a variety of ways in which the money can be applied: it might pay for facilities and equipment or help defray the costs of a team's taking part in a national or international event.

As well as being devoted players and supporters of football, Brazilians are very keen on many other kinds of sport, especially tennis, swimming, gymnastics, basketball, golf, sailing, boxing, horse-racing, rowing and athletics. They have provided international sport with world-famous champions like Esther Bueno, Emerson Fittipaldi and the great showjumper Nelson Pessoa.

Some baseball is played in Brazil, mainly by descendants of Japanese and American families in São Paulo. Cricket and Rugby football have been played for many years by British residents but they are not sports which have attracted Brazilians either as players or spectators.

Horse-racing is very popular in Rio, São Paulo and the South

and some of the race-tracks are beautifully laid out and equipped. There are no bookmakers or tic-tac men since all betting
is on the tote. Winning owners retain their prize-money in full
because percentages to trainers and jockeys as well as jockeys'
riding fees are paid by the Jockey Club.

Improved earnings, roads, accommodation and travel
facilities are enabling more and more Brazilians to indulge in
recreational activities which twenty years ago did not exist or,
if they did, were beyond the pockets of all but a few well-to-do
families. Mountain resorts and glorious beaches are now within
relatively easy reach of city dwellers who want to 'get away
from it all'. Boating and water-skiing are becoming popular
recreations, especially along the coast between Rio and Santos.

The limitation on the enjoyment of many recreational facilities in Brazil is the fact that it is often necessary to join a club
in order to take advantage of them. The usual system is that
members have to buy shares in the club and pay monthly
subscriptions as well. There are many fashionable clubs which
provide first-class facilities, but the cost of belonging to them is
extremely high. Shares in clubs can cost several hundreds of
pounds, but it must be admitted that they can generally be
passed on at a profit when the holders relinquish their member-
ship. Clubs usually profit from such exchanges by means of
transfer fees which sometimes exceed the value of the shares
themselves.

Large numbers of Brazilians have, like the Americans and
the British, a gambling streak in them and for about eighty
years they have been indulging this attribute—or failing—by
playing the *bicho* game. A source of gain for some and despair
for the large majority, it cannot be classified as a sport but has
certainly been a means of recreation for millions of people in the
country.

The dictionary classifies *bicho* as worm, grub, animal, but in
Brazilian Portuguese the word has much wider connotations.
In the sixteenth century a dreaded malady was 'sickness of the
bicho' which was described by travellers and physicians as a
'corruption of the intestines'. Brazilian Indians treated it with

suppositories made from pieces of lemon and green peppers, the effects of which are awful to contemplate. Anthony Knivet, an English sailor from Thomas Cavendish's fleet who was captured and held prisoner by the Portuguese in Brazil towards the end of the sixteenth century, recorded that the *bicho* sickness was 'common in all hot countries' and 'our English on the coasts of Brazil and Guinea' had died from it. Later it was found that a glassful of Brazilian *cachaça* (white rum), taken first thing every morning, was a good preventive of the *bicho* sickness and its regular use certainly reduced incidence of the complaint quite dramatically. A German named Seidler, who served as a lieutenant with the Brazilian imperial army, published a book in 1835 about Brazil in which he made this curious reference to the daily rum-drinking habit: 'As is the custom here, one first worthily kills the *bicho* in order that one can then hear Mass with maximum contrition.' A '*bicho*-killer' has become the slang expression for 'a tip' in the Brazilian language.

The *bicho* game became as prevalent as the 'sickness of the *bicho*' had been in former times. Probably the most honestly run illegal game of chance there is, it was soon an integral part of Brazilian day-to-day life. The whole thing was started by Barão de Drummond in early 1893, soon after Brazil had become a republic. He owned a property with a zoological garden near Rio. When the federal grant for the maintenance of the zoo animals was cut, the enterprising baron introduced a game of chance for those buying entrance tickets to his zoo. The gamble was to guess which out of twenty-five pictures of *bichos* the baron had selected and placed in a sealed sack the evening before. The pictures were of all sorts of creatures such as an ostrich, a dog, a butterfly, a snake, a monkey and so on, and each of the twenty-five *bichos* was given a number. People flocked to the baron's zoological garden for a gamble and soon the game spread throughout the country. The winning number of the daily lottery was used to determine the *bicho* winner.

The game has never been made legal (except for a few months during the 1920s) nor has it ever ceased operating since having been started by the Barão de Drummond. Like a successful guerrilla movement it worked with the support of the people. Experts have claimed in the past that it would be illegal to legalise the game without either revoking part of the law of penal infringements or altering the constitution itself. Attempts to tamper with its illegal status are considered to be an offence against Brazilian virtue, on the grounds that anyone who tries to make officially permissible something which is generally acknowledged to be morally wrong is making an attack on virtue itself. There is a similar attitude in Brazil towards divorce, which is also not allowed.

A group of so-called 'bankers' are the powers who run the game and working for them is a veritable army of *cambistas* or bookmakers who at one time were said to number 50,000 in the state of Rio de Janeiro alone. Near the centre of the web are the inner-circle agencies referred to as *fortalezas* (fortresses). In the days when the *bicho*-game organisation was really powerful, it easily survived police action which could only suppress some of its activities some of the time. The organisation was seriously weakened when the authorities took vigorous action against it in 1968, and even more so two years later when many *bicho* players began putting their money on the newly introduced football pools instead. Nevertheless, the game continues. One of its hallowed traditions is that winners are always paid in full, and this is rather remarkable when one considers that players have nothing more than a small scrap of paper to show that they have taken part in a game which is in any case illegal. Welshing would be an attack on virtue, no doubt.

Regular players know the *bichos* and their numbers off by heart, but beginners at the game have to learn the following list of the twenty-five *bichos* and the numbers allocated to them. It will be seen that each *bicho* has its own *grupo* (number) as well as four sets of two-digit numbers called *dezenas* (tens).

Grupo			Dezenas
1	Ostrich	(*Avestruz*)	01–02–03–04
2	Eagle	(*Aguia*)	05–06–07–08
3	Donkey	(*Burro*)	09–10–11–12
4	Butterfly	(*Borboleta*)	13–14–15–16
5	Dog	(*Cachorro*)	17–18–19–20
6	Goat	(*Cabra*)	21–22–23–24
7	Sheep	(*Carneiro*)	25–26–27–28
8	Camel	(*Camelo*)	29–30–31–32
9	Snake	(*Cobra*)	33–34–35–36
10	Rabbit	(*Coelho*)	37–38–39–40
11	Horse	(*Cavalo*)	41–42–43–44
12	Elephant	(*Elefante*)	45–46–47–48
13	Cock	(*Galo*)	49–50–51–52
14	Cat	(*Gato*)	53–54–55–56
15	Alligator	(*Jacaré*)	57–58–59–60
16	Lion	(*Leão*)	61–62–63–64
17	Monkey	(*Macaco*)	65–66–67–68
18	Pig	(*Porco*)	69–70–71–72
19	Peacock	(*Pavão*)	73–74–75–76
20	Turkey	(*Peru*)	77–78–79–80
21	Bull	(*Touro*)	81–82–83–84
22	Tiger	(*Tigre*)	85–86–87–88
23	Bear	(*Urso*)	89–90–91–92
24	Deer	(*Veado*)	93–94–95–96
25	Cow	(*Vaca*)	97–98–99–00

All sorts of happenings and situations inspire dedicated players in their selection of which *bicho* to play on. After attending a funeral they have the macabre habit of betting on the last two figures of the grave number. Some sleep with their feet tied together in order to dream of the quadrupeds or with their hands tied to inspire visions of the winged *bichos*. There is even the *bicho* player's *Prayer of the Nine Blessed Souls* which is more or less as follows:

Help me, my Holy Blessed Souls: the three who died burned, the three who died drowned, the three who died lost. And come all nine to tell me in a clear dream which bicho *will win tomorrow. My Holy Blessed Souls, let the three, the six and the nine get together and with the powers of God and of His Holy Mother give me in a clear dream tomorrow's* bicho *without hindrance or confusion. Pray three Hail Marys until You show me.*

Winners on the single *grupo* number are paid at the odds of 20 to 1 and on the two-digit *dezenas* at 70 to 1. One can play, if bolder, on the *centena* (100) by putting any number from 9 to 0 before the two-digit *dezena* of a *bicho* selection or on the *milhar* (1,000) by putting two numbers before the *dezena*. Winners on the *centena* are paid out at 700 to 1 and on the *milhar* at 5,000 to 1. Many players have a touching faith in the occurrence of miracles.

The following story illustrates the kind of disappointment which *bicho* players can experience. One day a hen in the town of Cantagalo (Cock's Crow) in the state of Rio de Janeiro laid an egg with what was clearly a number 5 on it. The news spread like wildfire through the town and the neighbouring districts. All players were convinced that Providence had sent the egg to indicate the *bicho* winner of that day. Number 5 corresponds to the dog and so all and sundry placed a bet on the dog with every cruzeiro they could scrape together. Bookmakers began to panic as the flow of money for number 5 became an avalanche: financial ruin would face them if the 5 came up. But life is full of surprises. It was not the dog that won but number 13 which is the cock. The losers quickly realised how wrongly they had interpreted the sign. After all, the hen, the egg and the name of the town should have been enough indication, they said ruefully.

HOLIDAYS

Since World War II a great change has taken place in the attitude of the average Brazilian towards holidays. A week at the seaside or at one of the numerous spas may still be the

holiday pattern for many of the people, but a large number
are beginning to range much farther afield. It is not air travel
so much as excellent bus services and the increased ownership
of private cars which altered the picture. It is now easy and
relatively inexpensive for Brazilians to travel by bus to Uruguay
or Argentina on scheduled services or package tours. Many
Brazilians travel far and wide within their own frontiers in
order to get to know their own country. Those who like to
combine this with a sea voyage take one of the periodic cruises
in a Brazilian ship from Santos all along the coast to Manaus
and back, a pleasant way of seeing cities of the North and North-
east as well as the river Amazon. The standard of hotels and
motels has been greatly improved to cater for the new wave of
travel and tourism in Brazil, and more accommodation becomes
available every year to meet rising holiday demands. At the
same time, credit facilities are being made available for costs of
holidays.

Camping holidays are a comparatively recent innovation in
Brazil but now that the idea has caught on, sites are being established at most of the beauty spots. Equipment is readily available
in the shops, and tents are becoming more and more in evidence
on the beaches and in the mountains although caravans are
rarely to be seen.

Not much given to peace and quiet, most Brazilians like to
spend their holidays in places where there is plenty of com-
panionship, activity and noise. They are gregarious by nature.
The scale of noise and pollution in the main cities is growing
so fast, however, that more and more families will probably
decide to adopt the policy of 'getting away from it all' during
their holidays. Already the Paulistas are beginning to 'discover'
quiet spots in the Cantareira hills, where they can build weekend houses and enjoy periodic rests away from the bustle of the
city. Estate agents advertise remote mountain properties in
the state of Rio as 'ideal for the practice of mental hygiene'.
Such holiday retreats can be acquired only by the wealthier
classes, however; and the majority of Brazilians, when planning
their holidays, are obliged to keep within limited budgets.

9

Hints for Visitors

REGULATIONS governing the entry of foreign tourists to Brazil have been eased during the past few years and visitors can expect no difficulties over passport or customs controls. Formalities for those wishing to settle permanently in Brazil are much stricter, however, and anyone considering such a step would be well advised to consult a Brazilian embassy or consulate for information about requirements and procedures.

Visitors will find that Brazilians are friendly and courteous to foreigners and ready to be as helpful as possible. Ask a Brazilian for directions and he will go to endless trouble to ensure that the visitor is put on the right road. Treat him with politeness and a smile and he is your friend. Brazilians are responsive and like to know where a visitor is from and what he thinks of Brazil. They like to hear good things but recoil at obvious flattery.

PORTERAGE

Service in hotels and restaurants is generally good. A service charge is usually added to bills but it is customary to give a little extra as a mark of appreciation if the service has been good. Some hotels leave all tipping to the discretion of their guests, a practice which many foreign visitors find rather trying, especially if they are unaccustomed to the local currency. If in doubt when the bill is presented, it is as well to ask whether a

L

service charge has been included. Petrol-station attendants are usually given a small tip when oil and tyres are checked on request but not for just filling up the tank. Taxi-drivers are generally tipped by being paid the nearest round figure to the fare shown on the meter, eg 4 cruzeiros if 3·70 is shown. Foreigners with scant knowledge of the country and little command of the language will nearly always find that they are treated with impeccable honesty where change is concerned but, as everywhere, there are exceptions to the rule.

Porterage charges at bus-stations and airports are mostly well controlled, with a set rate per item carried, but unfortunately the same does not always apply to railway travel. A traveller in the luxury night-train between Rio and São Paulo is expected to give a small tip to the cabin attendant but, when it comes to the question of railway porters to carry his baggage on and off the train, a foreigner may well find that outrageous sums are asked for these services. Porters making these demands usually plead great age and physical strain imposed by the carrying of luggage of apparently monstrous weight, but they usually have sufficient strength left at the end to accept about half the original price demanded for their exertions.

Supplements are charged for cabins on sleeper trains, but the price is small for the extra comfort obtained. Railway travel is reasonably cheap and it is possible to make a journey of many hours or even several days at a much lower comparative cost than is possible in the USA or in Britain.

BUS TRAVEL

Buses now provide the most popular means of transport in Brazil and excellent services are operated all over the country. A measure of the amount of traffic carried is shown by the fact that one bus company alone operates regular services between Rio and São Paulo at half-hourly intervals, with a break of only three hours during the day and night. Schedule punctuality is good. Journeys by sleeper bus cost more but the extra space inside these vehicles allows passengers, after they have been plied by the stewardess with sweets, biscuits and soft drinks, to let down the seats, stretch out and get a comfortable night's sleep.

AIR TRAVEL

There are different price tariffs for domestic air travel, depending on the type of aircraft and the schedule. The quickest and most expensive flights are the tariff-one jet, whereas cheaper and slower ones may put down several times at intermediate places before reaching their final destination. The slowest of all, which seem to call everywhere on their route, are called *pinga-pinga* (drop-drop) by the Brazilians. Free drinks and meals are served on the longer flights and coffee, fruit juice and snacks on the short hauls. Service on board is invariably willing and cheerful. Visitors with air tickets out of either Rio or São Paulo should find out beforehand whether their flights leave from the city or the international airport as the distance between them is considerable.

HOTELS

During the last ten years many hotels of international luxury class have been built in Brazil, especially in Rio and São Paulo, and new ones are under construction. The average price for a double room is £10 (about US $25) to include a continental breakfast with fruit; but a room in Rio with air-conditioning and facing the beach can cost nearly double this figure. In some cases, however, the higher price may include one meal (lunch or dinner); but this is not a system which is commonly found. In several hotels the breakfast will include not only oranges, bananas and pawpaw, but also cheese and slices of cold ham.

Visitors to Brasilia and nearly all state capitals and resorts can stay at hotels providing high standards of comfort and service at international prices, but adequate accommodation is not easily found by those who wander off the beaten track. Small hotels and boarding-houses in some of the remoter places at least have the merit of being cheap even if their standard of comfort leaves something to be desired. It is possible, for example, to stay at a small hotel in a town on the banks of the river Amazon for £3 (about US $7·50) which includes a bed for the night and all meals. Prices will be even cheaper in a frontier village or town but in many of these places a visitor will discover that he has to sleep in a hammock. Hammocks are a great boon to travellers in the Brazilian backlands for they are light to carry, comfortable to sleep in once the technique of body positioning has been mastered, easy to sling and unsling and they keep the occupant away from any dangers which may be lurking on the ground.

TOURIST ATTRACTIONS

Brazil has many attractions for visitors, including coast and countryside, modern cities and historic towns. Distance and travel-time usually prevent short-term visitors from seeing as much of the country as they would like to, however, and selectivity has to be practised. Many visitors who arrive in Rio confess to a somewhat vague yearning to 'see something of the Amazon', but they are often shaken to discover that a round trip of about 4,000 miles would be involved. Air travel and disregard for its cost naturally make an enormous difference to the number of places which visitors can see. It is perfectly feasible to catch an early-morning flight from Rio to Brasilia, have lunch there, see the layout and the architecture of the city and fly back to Rio in time for dinner. But the return air flight will cost over £40 (about US $100). Visitors to the charming old city of Salvador in Bahia, usually like to spend a few days there in order to see the churches and museums, try out delicious regional dishes, browse round the fascinating Modelo market, attend Macumba sessions, enjoy the wonderful beaches, admire the colonial architecture and absorb the special atmosphere of the city. There are glorious beaches farther north at Recife, Natal and Fortaleza and each of these cities has its own particular character and charm.

Within a short distance of the modern, bustling city of Belo Horizonte there are fascinating old mining towns where narrow cobbled streets contrast with the state capital's wide *avenidas*. Probably the best known of these is Ouro Preto, a gem of colonial and baroque architecture which was declared a national monument in 1933. There are beautiful churches to see as well as fine museums including one of mineralogy and precious stones. Women are often piqued to find that their handbags have to be deposited at the entrance to this museum, just in case the sight of some of the glorious stones on display should prove overwhelming. A feature of Ouro Preto is the small army of youths who offer their services as guides. They have a competent and sympathetic knowledge of their hometown and its treasures and are well worth employing for the small sum they charge. There are several places to stay at which provide modern comforts in an eighteenth-century atmosphere. Few visitors leave Ouro Preto without acquiring pieces of the locally made soapstone handwork on sale at most of the shops.

In the bay of Sepetiba, about two hours' journey south from Rio, there are beautiful islands with crisp sandy beaches lapped by a gentle and inviting sea against a background of warm sun and splendid scenery. Even the least lyrical of travel agents would describe the area as a tropical paradise. Undiscovered for many years, this part of the country is now developing as the new coast road between Rio and Santos nears completion. Already there are hotels on the islands of Itacuruçá and Jaguanum and it is only a question of time before more are built. Speedboats and water-skiers skim over waters where English pirates of the eighteenth century waited to attack the ships leaving Parati with gold brought down the mountains on muleback from the mines of Minas Gerais; or past the island where the Jesuits are said to have buried some of their treasure when the Order was expelled from Brazil. Farther south along the coast to Santos there are other sea resorts which are more easily reached from São Paulo, the most popular one being Guarujá. To the east of Rio there are great beach attractions at Cabo Frio and nearby Buzios, which are fashionable retreats for people living in Rio.

Those who visit Rio for the annual carnival should remember that it takes place during what is usually one of the warmest periods of the year and light clothes are therefore essential. When taking part in the festivities it is as well to carry little money because pickpockets operate among the crowds in conditions which favour them. Hardened carnival campaigners maintain that the only safe place for carrying money is in one's shoes, but this practice can lead to some discomfort after several hours of dancing. It is also rather a bore to have to remove one's shoes every time a bill is to be paid.

Visitors with time to travel inland will find it very worth while to visit the tremendous Iguazú Falls, greater than Niagara, which are situated in the state of Paraná where Brazil, Argentina and Paraguay come together. For sheer grandeur, the Iguazú Falls are unsurpassed. They can be reached by road or by air and there is hotel accommodation available only a short distance from them.

Those wanting to do some fishing in the interior of Brazil can take an organised tour in a botel operating along the beautiful river Araguaia through the home territory of the Karajá Indians. It is also possible to make an interesting boat journey lasting several days along the river São Francisco which will give the traveller an unusual look at the Brazilian countryside and a close view of riverside life and activities. Indian villages cannot be visited except with permission from the National Indian Foundation, and such permission is usually not given to those who wish to visit the Indians merely out of a sense of curiosity.

LOCAL CUSTOMS

Visitors to the country soon get used to the Brazilian custom of drinking a number of *cafezinhos* (little coffees) during the day. The small cup of black coffee is always offered to those visiting homes or offices and to accept it is a mark of politeness. This is no hardship since the *cafezinho* is usually delicious. Its appearance during very formal calls generally means that honour has been done and that the visitor can feel free to take his departure soon afterwards.

Brazilians like to shake hands both on meeting and on parting and foreigners are well advised to do so on every possible occasion. Conversation on first acquaintance is conducted rather formally in the third person, but this is soon replaced by the more familiar and infinitely easier form of *vôce* for you. It now becomes much simpler for the foreigner to say to a Brazilian professor, for instance: 'Would you and your wife care to have dinner with me?' rather than 'Would the professor and his wife care to have dinner with me?' Male friends greet each other with a preliminary handshake followed by an *abraço* (embrace). The technique of giving a friendly *abraço* can be learned only with experience since the manner of its execution may depend upon the occasion and the degree of friendship between the two people. Thus an *abraço* may take the form of an enveloping bear-hug to mark something special or a gentle clasp for more ordinary occasions.

A Brazilian man usually kisses the hand of a woman when he greets her, but a foreigner unaccustomed to this practice should not feel obliged to follow it and indeed he would be better advised to rely instead upon the polite handshake. Brazilian women usually greet each other with a kiss on both cheeks if the two are well acquainted and a man, if he knows the woman well, is permitted to do the same. However, this practice is generally reserved for relatives or close friends and the foreigner should be wary about taking such a liberty.

Visitors should be careful about the prices of certain services and commodities in Brazil. For example, car hire is extremely expensive and indeed it has been claimed that the prices charged are among the highest in the world. Petrol is not cheap and the octane value of even the best-quality *azul* (blue) is low

compared with high-grade fuel sold in the USA and the UK.
Brazilian-made cars are expensive; and customs charges and
dues on imported cars are prohibitive.

MEALS AND DRINKS

Meals and drinks in smart restaurants in big cities like Rio
and São Paulo are expensive by most international standards,
and £7 (about US $17·50) may be charged for a bottle of
unpretentious imported wine served with a meal. Visitors
intending to drink imported whiskies and liqueurs would be
wise to find out the price beforehand, otherwise they may get a
shock when they come to pay the bill. One guest in a São
Paulo hotel who asked for a bottle of Black Label whisky to be
sent up to his room was presented with a bill for £28 (nearly
US $70) on the following day. By being carefully selective,
however, visitors will find that they can eat, drink and enjoy
themselves in pleasant surroundings at reasonable prices. There
is no problem about the use of credit cards since they are now
widely accepted in Brazil. Travellers' cheques are better cashed
in banks rather than in shops, hotels and restaurants as the
rate given is usually better. Facilities for cashing cheques at
the official rate are also available at the main airports between
certain hours of business. Shops selling duty-free items do not
yet exist at the airports.

FORMS OF GREETING

Calling cards are widely used in Brazil and any visitor
intending to do business in the country should be equipped
with a good supply of them. If required they can be made
locally, at a reasonable cost, in a very short time. The same
applies to invitation cards.

Forms of greeting are *bom dia* (good-morning), for use up to
midday, *boa tarde* (good-afternoon) and *boa noite* which can be

used equally for 'good-evening' or 'good-night'. The usual way of saying good-bye after personal contact or on the telephone is *até logo* (until soon). The expression for 'Have a good trip' is *Boa viagem*. The parting wish of Brazilians to friends leaving their country is: 'Have a good trip and come back soon', which in Portuguese is *Boa viagem e breve regresso*.

Acknowledgements

THE author is indebted to many officials, official departments and private individuals for the information and encouragement they provided. In particular he wishes to thank Minister Themístocles Brandão Cavalcanti, Ambassador Alarico Silveira Junior of the Brazilian Ministry of External Affairs and the Fundação IBGE Instituto Brasileiro de Estatística. His special thanks are due to the directors of the magazine *Manchete*, of Rio de Janeiro, for having kindly allowed their photographs to be used, including that reproduced on the jacket.

Index